The Trainee Teacher's Survival Guide

Also available in the series

How to Survive your First Year in Teaching – Sue Cowley

Guerilla Guide to Teaching – Sue Cowley

Inside Guide to Training as a Teacher – Jon Barbuti

The Trainee Teacher's Survival Guide

Hazel Bennett

continuum

Continuum International Publishing Group

The Tower Building
11 York Road
London
SE1 7NX

80 Maiden Lane
Suite 704
New York
NY 10038

British Library Cataloguing-in-Publication Data
A catalogue record for this book is available from the British Library.

ISBN: 978-0-8264-8507-3 (paperback)

Library of Congress Cataloging-in-Publication Data
A catalog record for this book is available from the Library of Congress.

Typeset by Servis Filmsetting Ltd, Manchester
Printed and bound in Great Britain by Biddles Ltd,
King's Lynn, Norfolk

Contents

Acknowledgements

I should like to thank the following teachers for their help in compiling this book:

Katrina Beciri, Russell Bennett, Steve Bloom, Jim Daly, Carole Edwards, Adam Haffner, Shirin Haidari, Claire Hart, Sorana Leach, Emma Laikin, Cecilia McKeague, Helen Pallet, Kevin Paradise, Philip Rosenthal and Elaine Wilson

With special thanks to Kate Nivison, for her expert guidance.

1 Preparation for Training

Why Be a Teacher?

The teaching profession offers the opportunity to make a major contribution to the quality of life of the nation's children, in fact, its future. Grateful pupils remember competent teachers for the rest of their lives and the job offers levels of satisfaction and pleasure which for many teachers outweighs having to accept a lower salary than some other professions.

But do note – choosing the right career for you is so important because the wrong choice can result in a loss of precious time and energy. In the past the cynical saying, 'Those who can, do. Those who can't, teach' did have a grain of truth in it as some people only went into teaching after being turned down by their first choice of career. Some people drift into teaching, after university in particular, because they are not sure what to do with their working life.

The course is intensive and time-consuming and so it is important not to enter it unless you are absolutely certain that teaching is your chosen career.

I have been told by a few students that the generous training salary for graduates was a deciding factor for some. I am of course in favour of paying graduates a training salary, because the profession needs new blood and the thought of chalking up another year's worth of debt, without a reasonably high initial salary to make it worthwhile, may deter potential teachers. However, the training salary alone is not an adequate reason to choose teaching.

If you believe anything you have heard about teaching being a nice, comfortable little job – short hours, long holidays – forget it. The contact hours, i.e. time actually spent with pupils, can be shorter than most jobs – about 28 hours per week – but they can be intensely pressurized. There are also hours of preparation, in addition to tedious hours of marking, record keeping, report writing, looking for lost coats/PE kits, as well as placating irate or anxious parents, after-school clubs, open evenings, staff meetings and school journeys.

If you think the holidays are a compensation for the above, you may well find that it sometimes takes a chunk of the holidays to unwind. Moreover you may not have enough money to go anywhere interesting in comfort for a few years, unless your partner or parents are prepared to subsidize it.

Women may find that people who have never taught will tell you, it's 'a good job for a woman'. By this they mean that you can leave work at 4pm, pick up your own children, and have plenty of time to put the dinner on the table for your husband who has 'done a day's work'. It's nonsense of course. It's difficult to leave at 4pm because of all the extra tasks and meetings to attend.

Another consideration might be that if you have children of your own, you may feel that you can never escape from children. Unless you have a bottomless pit of patience, you might suffer higher stress levels than childless teachers, or parents who can escape from their children by working with adults. Sometimes you will only be able to cope by arriving at school early, around 7.30am, working through breaks and lunch hours and taking work home where it might be difficult to do it because you are beset by demands from your own children.

Teachers themselves sometimes advise their children not to become teachers, although I notice that the advice is rarely accepted.

Nevertheless, if you are energetic, creative, enjoy a challenge, are competent at communicating ideas enthusiastically and have a talent for forming easy relationships with a wide range of people, read on. Teaching could well be the perfect job for you.

Choosing the Right Course

There are now more channels into teaching than ever before.

- Bachelor of Education Degree course (B.Ed.) which gives you four years of teacher training and a qualification which carries Qualified Teacher Status (QTS).

- A degree in any subject and then acquire teacher training and QTS by doing a one-year (or about 40 weeks excluding the summer holiday) Post-Graduate Certificate in Education (PGCE).
- Graduate Teacher Training Programme (GTTP) – graduates work in a school and attend college for an academic year (about 40 weeks).
- School Centred Initial Teacher Training (SCITT) course. These are run by Local Education Authorities (LEAs).
- Bachelor degree courses, e.g. BA with Educational Studies, but these must be followed by another year of teacher training to get QTS.

Your choice of course will depend on which suits your family commitments, your finances and your present qualifications. If you are still at school or if you only have A-levels, you will be choosing between B.Ed., a degree and PGCE, or degree and then the GTTP.

To help you make up your mind, you might like to consider the following points.

- Are you absolutely committed to teaching as a career, or would you like to keep your options open in case you change your mind? Some universities give you the chance to opt out of teaching during the course and you can still finish with a BA degree.
- Is money a problem? If so you may just have to choose the course which makes it convenient for you to live at home.
- What do you most want from the your higher education? Do you want to study your chosen subject(s) in depth or would you prefer to spend more time acquiring teaching experience and learning the technicalities of it. For the former you might choose a degree and then a year of PGCE or GTTP, and a B.Ed. for the latter.
- How do you yourself learn best? Some students love the study aspect of the course and enjoy immersing themselves in books to extend their knowledge and understanding of the philosophical aspect of teaching, and so they might prefer the B.Ed. option. Others who learn more quickly from practical

experience are more likely to prefer the degree and PGCE or GTTP option.

- Do you thrive on pressure? The PGCE and GTTP is probably the tougher option as you have to compress so much into under a year and learn quickly from your mistakes. If you prefer a less steep learning curve the B.Ed. is probably the more comfortable.
- PGCE and GTTP are for fast learners and you must be willing to learn quickly from your mistakes. With a B.Ed. you have more time to redo things and to put into practice what you have been taught or else improve upon what you have done. There are fewer opportunities to do this with a PGCE.

If you follow the B.Ed. option, you will have a longer period to concentrate on teaching *per se*. The PGCE and GTTP options are really only ten months of training after you exclude the summer holidays. They are very intensive and at the end some believe that you are possibly not as well prepared as the B.Ed. teachers, who have studied and trained for four years.

I believe that so much of your performance is reliant on your personal qualities of patience, creativity, understanding of pupils' difficulties, organizational skills, and ability to relate well to other people that the difference is not huge. By the time one has completed two terms of the induction year it is probable that any difference in the effect of the two courses will have evened out.

If you want to teach in a secondary school, having a degree in your chosen subject is very beneficial as you will be concentrating solely on that subject or allied subjects for the rest of your teaching career. A large body of knowledge and understanding are essential for a teacher who may be expected to teach up to A-level standard and of course the training salary for the PGCE is a tremendous bonus for those who want to start reducing their debts after graduation.

The graduate teacher training programme

This course differs from a PGCE in that it is school based. Graduates spend an academic year working mostly in school with some time in college. They have another placement of about four weeks in a different school so that they have a wider perspective of the range of schools in the UK.

This is an option often preferred by graduates who have done something else before deciding to join the teaching profession. This course allows you a lot of opportunity to practise your teaching skills but of course a lot less time to study the theory and less opportunity to reflect on successful practice and discuss issues with lecturers and other students.

As with the PGCE it is a steep learning curve as you have less than a year to learn everything which the B.Ed. student has to learn in four years, but of course it is reasonable to expect graduates to learn more quickly because they have already had the experience of completing a degree. On this course you can be thrown into the deep end fairly quickly.

The Right College or University

This is most important, particularly if you are starting a three- or four-year course, because if you make the wrong choice you are stuck with it. You need to be confident that you can feel happy in the atmosphere and there are plenty of other activities for you to enjoy because it is rare for teachers to bring about a change of course from one college to another.

It is vital to attend an open day at each of the colleges or universities to which you apply and make sure you talk to students who attend the college or have just left it because they can give you a greater insight into what it is really like, rather than a glossy brochure or any lecturer addressing the crowd of applicants.

Much of the advice which follows could apply to students contemplating any college or university course, not just teacher training. Draw up a list of the things which are important to you, taking into account each of the following.

The structure and content of the course itself

All teaching courses have to cover a core curriculum, but of course some will be specializing in certain subjects.

Does it contain enough of the subjects which interest you? Remember if you want to be a primary teacher, you will have to study a bit of every subject on the curriculum. A few hours spent studying the syllabus of each course is time well spent.

Support for the student

Most colleges and universities have student support services such as student counselling services, vocational guidance and a health centre.

Teacher training courses can be very tough if you are assigned to a challenging school for teaching practice. Finding yourself working with children who are socially disadvantaged through poverty, homelessness or distress in the home can be a severe shock to the system for students who have had little contact with social problems in their lives.

Most colleges take seriously their responsibility of supporting students who are given difficult classes without guidance on how to deal with them and will take steps to make sure the student is properly supported in the school. Don't be afraid to ask at your interview how often you will see your college supervisor while on teaching practice and how they would support you if you were having a hard time.

Prospects after qualifying

Don't forget there are college and university league tables publicizing what percentage of students get jobs after leaving. Since most colleges and universities advise students to look at school league tables before they apply for a job in a school, the same rule must apply to themselves. Obviously there is no point in spending a few years working hard unless there is a high chance of you getting a teaching job at the end of it.

The location of the college or university

If you are already married or have children or both, your priority will be to study somewhere close to home. This could severely limit your choice. If you have more than one relevant institution within reasonable travelling distance, you may have to balance up your real choice against the time spent on travelling. Always work out how much time is needed to do the journey in the rush hour. You could try a dummy run each way. Remember having two hours a day of unnecessary travelling will generate stress and lessen the quality of life for you and your family.

If you are young and single, it is often beneficial to leave home completely, money permitting. Coping on your own in a new place is a beneficial experience and competent teachers are usually independent people who can stand securely on their own two feet. People grow up more quickly when they are not depending on their parents for daily, moral and practical support.

The college environment
It's imperative that you like the feel of it. Environment has a strong effect on behaviour and mood and it would be disappointing to arrive and find your college in a dismal area with few amenities and poor public transport. When you go for your interview, make sure a detailed trip of the whole environment is included.

Don't forget to check the glossy pictures in the brochure against the reality of the campus. Remember that everywhere looks different on a wet day in winter, than on the sunny day in the photograph.

The wider environment
Look at the town or city and what it has to offer by way of culture and leisure activities. Large cities are usually brimming with interesting places to go, but if you are considering studying in a small town or suburban area, it is important to check the local transport for the evenings and weekends.

Also you need to check that it is a safe place to go out in the evenings. A small number are located in areas where it is foolish to go out at night on foot, even in a group. If you attend one of these it is imperative to have a car or enough money to pay regular taxi or minicab fares. This is not an exaggeration. I know one young student who with his friends suffered a senseless beating from a gang of thugs who did not bother to steal their wallets or mobile phones.

Accommodation
It is important to get this fixed up well in advance of starting your course, preferably with the help of your university. I have known students to have a miserable first term, frantically looking for affordable accommodation that is not slummy, and within reasonable travelling distance of their college. Some universities and colleges have enough accommodation in halls of residence for all of their students for the duration of their course, some for part of it. Try to find one that organizes accommodation for the first year at least, and enquire about how students find housing for the rest.

The advantages of living in college halls are that they are usually convenient to the college, geared up for the students' needs, and there are lots of students together so they make friends quickly. Many provide meals, which breaks you into your new life gently.

It is vitally important to ask to be shown around the college halls when you go for your interview because some are very old and dilapidated. I have known students to withdraw their application on seeing the college halls.

The extra-curricular facilities

Check the clubs and societies section of the brochure to ensure there are enough which interest you. Most have a wide variety.

Also look closely at their facilities. An athletics club will never be top rate unless they have a proper 400 metres stadium and field equipment, and a dramatic society is greatly enhanced by an attractive theatre with effective acoustics and up-to-date lighting and sound equipment. Remember that your job opportunities are greatly enhanced, especially for primary school, if you can provide music, drama and sports activities.

Funding

For many students today this is a headache. The days when students from lower income homes could happily go off to college or university secure in the knowledge that their student grant and earnings from holiday jobs would be sufficient to see them through the term are now long gone and today's students suffer from money problems which were unknown to my generation.

Paying fees

For most teacher training courses the university or college fees will be paid in full by the Local Education Authority (LEA). It is important to apply to your LEA in plenty of time to see if you are eligible for a grant to have your fees – or most of them – paid for you. You should telephone your LEA at the start of your A-level year and ask when it is necessary to have your application in.

When sending off an application form as vital as this, it is a sensible precaution to enclose a stamped addressed postcard to yourself, with the words 'Application for University fees', written on the back. If you slip in a note asking them to sign the postcard and return it, you can be absolutely certain it has arrived. This gives you peace of mind from knowing it has not been lost in the post.

Once they have agreed to pay your fees, that agreement lasts for the whole of your time at university, even if you move house to live in a different LEA.

Living expenses

Even if they take holiday jobs, most students have to take out a low-interest loan from the Student Loan Company to cover their living expenses. This does not have to be paid back until you start earning, and at least some of it may not have to be paid back at all if you are eligible for the Repayment of Teachers' Loans scheme.

The loan system has the disadvantage that students leave university with a mountain of debt around their neck, but nonetheless many students say it is better than having no university education at all.

A small number are fortunate enough to have parents who bankroll them for the duration of their course. If you are in this happy position it is a smart move to take out a loan anyway and invest the money in a tax-free Individual Savings Account (ISA) or Premium Bonds, keep the interest or winnings and pay the loan back at your leisure. This is perfectly legal but, if following this advice, it is sensible not to mention it to students who are struggling with finances because it is irritating for those who cannot do it.

In certain teaching jobs where there is a shortage, a fraction of the loan is wiped out each year that you teach in a maintained school and so you make an even greater gain.

Other students have parents who would like to help but are unable to do so. Sometimes they help by telling their sons or daughters to take out a loan and they will help them to pay it off when the time comes.

Financial help available for the student teacher

- A tax-free training bursary of £6,000 is available to most post-graduates on the PGCE course, who are resident in the UK. From August 2005, students training to teach secondary science and maths will have a training salary of £7,000. Neither of these has to be paid back.

- Post-graduate students who are undertaking a school based training like GTTP are paid a salary by their employer, the school, and it is usually about the same as an unqualified teacher – £13,000 in a maintained school, at the time of writing (2005). As a salary it is taxed. Independent schools who take on a GTTP student must pay the training fee and a similar taxable salary.
- The Secondary Shortage Subject Scheme (SSSS) (in England only). This is a means-tested, hardship fund of up to £6,000, though the full amount is rarely met.
- Help with childcare, travel and other course-related costs. For further details telephone the DfES information line 0800 731 9133.
- Welsh language incentive. Students in Wales should apply to their teacher training provider.
- Undergraduate courses in Wales. At the time of writing these include means-tested grants of up to £1,500 per year, a further £1,000 for secondary undergraduates to support them through their school placement if they are on priority subjects and £600 if they are on non-priority subjects.

Useful contact information
- www.tta.gov.uk/fundingfortrainees.
- DfES Student Support free information line 0800 731 9133.
- Teaching Information line 0845 6000 991 or 0845 600 992 for Welsh speakers.
- Your own LEA. Ask for the department for student support for student teachers.

Golden Hellos for teachers
This is a delightful bonus for eligible post-graduate teachers who have successfully completed their induction year and are teaching a shortage subject such as science, mathematics or ICT. When they enter their second year of teaching in a maintained school they receive a taxable but non-repayable bonus. At the time of writing the amount is £4,000. For more up-to-date information telephone the Teaching Information line 0845 6000 991 or 0845 6000 992 for Welsh speakers.

2 Getting onto the Course

Think Ahead

If you are still at school

Start your planning early by remembering that many colleges will not consider you unless you have some experience of working with children or teenagers. Have you been a Sunday school teacher, cub, scout or brownie leader or a youth worker in any local community centre? Did you have responsibility for running any school club or Combined Cadet activities? Have you been a captain of any sports club in school or out of it? These all show that you can take responsibility for organizing young people. Mentioning any of these on the form will enhance your chances of acceptance.

If you have done any of these things in school, it is worth writing them down and passing it, as an aide-memoire, to the person who writes your reference. They are unlikely to resent your doing so, in fact they will have so much to remember they will probably be glad of your help.

If you already have a degree

If you already have a degree and are applying for a place on a post-graduate course it is almost essential to have had some experience of working in a school. This means finding a friend who works in a school – it doesn't have to be a teacher – and contacting the head and asking if you can work in the school voluntarily for a week or two. It is easier if you have someone on the inside to introduce you because heads have got to be so careful about who they allow into their school.

Alternatively most universities have an afternoon each week with no lectures. Some undergraduates contact a local school and offer to spend that afternoon every week working there voluntarily.

This is sensible, not just to impress the selection panel, but to let you see that the classroom can look very different from the other side of the school desk. Many young people, particularly those who have attended well-equipped schools in affluent areas are unaware of the challenges presented in schools with high turnovers of staff because of the pressures of coping with large classes or high percentages of children with special needs, very little spoken English, or the obstacles to learning imposed by poverty, disturbance and distress in the home.

By mentioning your awareness of the extra challenges that schools face, you are demonstrating your insight into the issues involved in being a successful teacher. That is bound to impress.

I know several graduates, who before doing their one-year postgraduate study, actually worked full-time as unqualified teachers in private schools or international schools abroad. Obviously this was a safe passport onto the course.

Applying to the college/university

Don't limit yourself to one college or university: apply for several and wait for the conditional offers. You will probably have to apply through the Universities and Colleges Admissions Service (UCAS), but teachers in your school are able to advise you. When offers arrive it is tempting to put the lowest offer down as your first choice, but it really is better to put the one you really prefer first, because once you have put a college or university as first you are expected to take it even if you have good enough grades for the second.

Filling in the form

Often students are so keen to set the wheels in motion that they fill in the form and send it off without taking time to consider all the fine tuning.

Try to keep it at the front of your mind that universities are not scratching around looking for students to fill their places: they have far more applicants then they could possibly accommodate so you need to make your application as near to perfect as you possibly can, to maximize your chances.

- Always photocopy the form before you start and write a couple of practice copies before you write the one you intend to send off.
- This is the first impression they have of you so the form must be neat and word perfect. Typing, where possible, is best, unless the form says that it has to be in your own handwriting.
- Bear in mind that although supply and demand for college places is also a factor, no college will accept anyone they consider unsuitable just to fill up their places.
- If you are still at school your careers teacher should be willing to look over a draft of your application form before you write the final copy and send it off. They can often suggest small improvements.
- Keep a copy of the form to use in preparation for your interview and to have as a basis for filling in the next one.

The student's statement is the most important part. The selection panel are looking for students who are absolutely certain they want to be teachers. Say why you want to be a teacher – why you have enjoyed working with children or teenagers; who or what inspired you. You got satisfaction out of helping them to learn/progress/ develop skills. Mention that it has widened your horizon, making you more aware of the difficulties they face and given you the urge to make a difference.

The Interview

It is vital for the universities' and colleges' admissions panels to be certain that the students they accept are absolutely sure that they want to teach because they do not want their course statistics to be spoiled by a high drop-out rate. They look for evidence of commitment to the profession and lip-service is not enough. Some lecturers say that they are looking for students who have demonstrated commitment to children as well as their subject and are more likely to accept students who have experience of working with children or teenagers.

This is your chance to enlarge on all your experience of working with young people. They will like it if you speak enthusiastically, making it clear that you have benefited from the experience. Tell them what skills you have developed – organizing trips, coping with critical parents, teaching children to sort out conflicts, managing behaviour of children with problems, supporting them through anxiety about exams, adolescence, parents separating. You can't work with children for long without learning something from them and you should demonstrate this.

Similarly if you are a graduate, hoping to do a PGCE or GTTP next, the admissions panel will be impressed if you describe work that you have done successfully while working voluntarily in a school.

The interview panel is looking for potential teachers who also possess the following qualities, not necessarily in this order:

good health;
an even keener interest in children and teenagers than in their subject;
ability to sustain long hours of pressure;
inventiveness of mind;
self-confidence;
ability to stand up for oneself strongly but without aggression;
intelligence;
patience;
tolerance;
sensitivity;
ability to work cooperatively with adults and children of all classes, creeds, colours and levels of ability.

They have half-an-hour to find out how many of these qualities you possess, and you have half-an-hour to persuade them you have all or most of them.

A few guidelines
Interviews differ from college to college. In some they are very formal and you are quizzed by a small panel of lecturers. Others are quite informal and relaxed. Some students have told me that the interviewer appeared to be just trying to get to know them.

The following points may be helpful.

- Look smart. Even in these liberal times, many lecturers still think it is important. You can of course revert to a casual appearance for the rest of your college career, except teaching practice.

- Hold your head up and your shoulders back and look them confidently in the eye.
- If you are nervous, try to hide it. They are looking for self-assured people.
- Don't mumble. A clear voice that is pleasant to the ear is an important attribute for a teacher.
- Never fabricate or exaggerate your experience. If you are caught out, you will definitely be turned down.

Preparation

You should always prepare for an interview because there is nothing more disheartening than coming out of an interview and thinking of answers you could have given. Before you go you should ask yourself what questions you would ask if you were the interviewer. Forewarned is fore-armed. If you know people who have recently had similar interviews, ask them what questions they were asked and prepare by writing down the questions and adding model answers.

Ask a friend to take your notes and give you a practice interview the night before. I always find this preparation enhances my performance for any sort of interview. Read your notes an hour or less before you go in. Here are a few questions to practise. You can choose the answer you think best or prepare your own.

Q   Why do you want to be a teacher?
A   I have a keen interest in children/the promotion of skills and knowledge.

   I want a rewarding job.

   I once had a superb teacher, who was so enthusiastic and was clearly thriving on her success, she inspired me to enter the profession.

   Teaching is in my family, so I do know all the drawbacks as well as the good points.
Q   What is your experience of children?
A   I have worked with youth groups, Sunday school, holiday play schemes, sports clubs, Combined Cadets. (They may pick something interesting out of your application form. This is your chance to elaborate on everything you have done.)

A   I have children of my own, babysat for others, got loads of younger brothers, sisters, cousins.

Q   How has this influenced your decision to be a teacher?

A   I enjoy working with them.

I take pleasure in watching them learn, develop, mature, acquire new skills.

Although my parents who are teachers complain about the stresses and strains of the job, I notice that they also get a lot of pleasure out of it and don't seem to want to give it up.

Q   What skills/qualities does a teacher need?

An inventive mind, the ability to cope with people of all sorts, organizational skills, a wide body of knowledge (primary), a deep knowledge and understanding of their subject (secondary), patience (all age groups), enthusiasm, endurance, thick skin, ability to think ahead, think of several things at once, think on one's feet, flexibility.

Q   What is the more important, organizational skills or patience for pupils?

Organizational skills. If you are not well organized, it is easier for pupils to become disorganized/disinterested and then you will need even more patience to regain their attention.

Or

Patience. A good relationship with pupils is the bedrock of successful teaching. Pupils need above all to know that their teachers care about them, have the time and patience to listen to them.

(A lecturer will not mind you having a different opinion to him/herself as long as you can back it up with logical reasoning.

Q   What are your leisure time activities? (They should be on the form.)

A   Have a long list ready. They are looking for all round people. Expand on your answer by telling them why it is such a valuable skill. For example, if you have a talent for music, point out how it makes you use both halves of the brain. If you are keen on sports elaborate on the health aspect. Explain how you could use your knowledge and skills in school, e.g. for extra-curricular activities.

Q How do you think you will cope with being alone with children for most of a working day?

A I shall enjoy the challenge.

(Although it is fashionable, I hate that word 'challenge'. It's the current buzzword to cover the panacea of all ills.)

Or

I find it fascinating to watch them interacting and developing.

Q How would you inspire a love of your subject in your pupils? (Secondary)

A Build up a positive relationship with them and make sure I deliver lessons which are interesting and involve them in active learning.

Try to make the subject relevant to them and to what interests them. For example, maths teachers can make up problems about calculating angles on a football pitch, English teachers make sure they make available plenty of books which appeal to the pupils' age group. History comes alive when children visit historical sites and take part in historical activities. Introduce drama into lessons, children love to perform and have everyone's attention.

Q When did you last read/how well informed are you about the National Curriculum document for your subject? (secondary).

If you are still at school, you could ask one of your teachers to lend you a copy of the document to read before your interview. (If you have left school you can acquire them from DfES orderline, Sanctuary Buildings, Great Smith Street, London SW1 3BT. Telephone 0845 602 2260. www.dfes.gov.uk.

Q Why is the National Curriculum important?

A It provides some uniformity within the system, so that pupils going off to secondary school have had a similar foundation for their secondary teachers to build upon. It also ensures that schools do not leave blank spots in their pupils' knowledge, even though some schools may be able to achieve a higher standard than others.

Q What aspects of the National Curriculum do you find stimulating/unstimulating?

A Whatever your main subject, you could adapt a few of these or think up your own:

I like parts that involve the pupil finding out things for themselves, e.g. planning and carrying out science experiments, reading historical documents, maths investigations.

I like National Curriculum topics which are relevant to normal everyday life, like studying man's effect on the environment and the need to conserve the earth's resources.

Learning languages is so satisfying because it enables you to get more out of your holidays abroad if you can communicate with the people.

I like topics which involve hands-on activities like recycling paper in the classroom, visiting museums or villages (like Blist's Hill Victorian village) where pupils have the opportunity to experience a past way of life are tremendously stimulating.

I am not so keen on topics which are purely theoretical and don't seem relevant to me and my everyday life, e.g. I have learnt lots of topics in maths which I cannot use.

You can add a philosophical comment about the impossibility of producing a National Curriculum which would stimulate all pupils in all topics and realizing you have to cope with it all, stimulating or not.

Sometimes they give a group of applicants a piece to read and then they have a group discussion about the article with a lecturer there to supervise. This can be difficult as some people will try to get themselves noticed by dominating the discussion, excluding others. Fortunately lecturers are aware of this and are able to give all the students the chance to express their opinions. If you find yourself taking part in this sort of activity, don't be afraid to speak up. It doesn't matter whether the lecturer agrees with you or not. They want to know if you have got ideas, confidence and can show that you are a thinking person.

When the A-level results come out
As with any university application it is vital to be at home or at least within immediate computer access when the results come out. Remember you may need to go to an interview at short notice so if you really cannot be at home you should not be far away or at the

very least within Easyjet/Ryanair or other budget airline travelling distance.

Don't despair if you do not have the grades for your preferred college. You must log on to the website immediately to find out if you have been accepted anyway because often, if they have enough places, they will take students with a lesser grade, especially if they have had a successful interview. If not, you can telephone them quickly and tell them you are still interested. They will tell you if there is any chance and you will have to either wait in hope for a day or two or contact Clearing House.

Clearing House is an organization whose job is to match up students who want to go to university with the places still available. If you have reasonably good results and are willing to be flexible about where you go, you may very well still get a place if you follow their procedure. Their home page is www.hero.ac.uk/uk/home/index.cfm. For clearing instructions go to www.ucas.com/clearing/instr.html. For a list of colleges and universities and their contact details which you can, of course, contact directly without Clearing House, go to www.ucas.com/clearing/instlist.html. For a list of frequently asked questions go to www.ucas.com/clearing/quest.html.

If you have got the right grades, you must contact the college or university at once to accept the place.

The Pre-Course Placement

If you are a graduate and you have been accepted for the GTTP or PGCE course your college may ask you to spend a week in a school before you start your teacher training. This is to give you the chance to make absolutely certain you like it, to get the feel of the job and hopefully pick up a few tips.

The pre-course placement is time well spent because some people decide after a week of grief that it is not for them, and so save themselves a lot of trouble. I know one graduate who withdrew her application from the course because she was deterred by the staffroom politics alone. Unfortunately, some do not discover that teaching is not their cup of tea until they have gone a term or two into the course, causing wasted time and effort all round.

You will have to organize this for yourself. The best way is through a teacher whom you know, but if you do not know any who you feel you can approach, just try a few schools in your area and ask. It is sensible to call in at the school and ask in person if you can spend a week there because heads understandably can be wary of allowing strangers in. It's a good idea to bring your college's letter with you, partly so that the head knows what they want you to do and partly for identification. If the head has any doubts s/he can telephone the college.

Most schools are amenable to allowing a potential teacher to spend a week with them and some are only too happy to welcome an extra pair of hands. Of course you must always dress smartly before you go, as first impressions are important.

On the placement week, some start to have doubts and are uncertain whether they should continue. If you find yourself in this position don't make a rash decision which you might later regret. Remember that there is a wide variety of primary and secondary schools and you might just have been unlucky. You could contact another school and ask to pass a week there.

Try to keep it at the front of your mind that there is no such thing as a typical school. There are private schools with small classes, the best equipment and supportive parents; and rough schools with a large number of challenges posed by poverty, low staffing levels and poor management. There is also every combination in between. A change of school might completely transform your view.

If you can, it is worth trying to spend longer than a week in a school and/or do some other type of work with children in a holiday play scheme or youth group. To do this you could ring up your LEA and ask if they run holiday play schemes or if they can tell you of any. You could also visit your local library to see what is available locally. Sometimes churches organize activities for children but these are voluntary and you might need something which pays.

Tips on coping with your placement
Keeping your path smooth
- As soon as you arrive go straight to the head to introduce yourself if you have not already met and thank her/him for allowing you to come.
- On the first day, wear something neutral in the clothes department and then adapt accordingly to the school's dress code

because it is irritating for teachers if they find that visitors can get away with something they can't.

- Ask fairly quickly whom to pay for tea and coffee and pay up front.
- Try to get on with everyone and avoid staffroom politics.
- Volunteering to do playground duty will improve your welcome.
- If they have any fund-raising or evening events that week, offer to turn up and help.
- Keep your negative comments to yourself. Teachers tend to withdraw their help quite quickly when you rub them up the wrong way.

Behaving like a professional

- You might hear staff talking about pupils. It is important to respect the confidentiality of all such information.
- Don't be afraid to ask about anything you don't understand. No one blames you for wanting to learn, but don't bombard teachers with questions.
- If a pupil makes a negative comment about a member of staff, you can sidestep by changing the subject. It is unwise to allow yourself to be drawn into an argument.
- Stay well out of any heated staffroom discussions.
- After you leave write a letter of thanks to the head and any teacher who has been particularly helpful.

Being sensitive to the teachers

- If the school is in the pre-Ofsted period, expect nothing from the teachers because they are under far too much pressure.
- If it is the post-Ofsted period, still expect nothing because they are completely shattered.

Understanding the background

If you plan to do the PGCE for teaching in a secondary school, you might be asked to do your placement in a primary school. This is really a good idea, because it gives you the chance to:

- get a feel for a primary school atmosphere so you know the children's previous experience;

- see the level of work that pupils can achieve at the top end of the primary school, to give you a better idea of what you can expect from them in their first year in secondary, remembering that this will vary from school to school;
- note the level of maturity of pupils at the top end of the primary school.

Remember that to teach in a secondary school, you need a wide range of personnel skills because you have to teach children, hormonal adolescents and young adults.

How to get the most out of the placement

It is now recognized that even experienced teachers learn a lot by observing the efficient practice of others. In fact, in some schools teachers are encouraged to spend some time in other classes observing their colleagues. You will be probably enjoy sitting in classrooms, observing how teachers work, picking up ideas and musing about how much it has all changed since you were at school.

Before you go into a classroom remember that some teachers, even competent, experienced ones, can be self-conscious and might not actually want you there. Try to be sensitive. If they seem less than pleased about your presence, it is worth making an admiring remark about the displays on the wall, asking if there is anything you can do to help or where it is most convenient for you to sit.

A positive, supportive attitude and willingness to work and learn go a long way with most teachers. And of course always thank them before you move on to the next class.

What to look for while observing a lesson

The staff–pupil relationship plays a large part in the quality of work for both the pupils and the teacher. Relationships reflect the personality of the head. Those heads who are efficient and treat the staff even-handedly and with appreciation, tend to have a staffroom full of people who extend the same goodwill to their colleagues and pupils. The set of rules by which the staff treat each other and the pupils is sometimes called the hidden curriculum. You might want to look at it as well as the teacher's behaviour management techniques and methods of organizing the class to learn. Try observing these points.

Managing the pupils
- Is the atmosphere calm, strained, pressurized, happy, hostile?
- Behaviour management skills – how does s/he control the pupils?
- Are the pupils switched on, on task, involved in the learning activities?
- If you look at a lesson where the pupils are not switched on and one where they are, ask yourself what causes the difference? Is it the lesson content, the way it is presented, the activities which the pupils do, the teacher's relationship with the pupils or a mixture of two or more of these?
- How does the teacher coax the less interested pupils to take part?

Delivering the lessons
- Look at the overall structure of lessons. Watch how the warm-up, main part of the lesson and plenary all fit together and flow into each other.
- How is the lesson organized – is the teacher doing all the work and the pupils sitting passively? Are they working independently, in groups cooperatively? Or is there a mixture of these?
- Are the pupils aware of the objective of the lesson and has the teacher achieved it?, i.e. have the pupils grasped the concept, developed the skill, do they understand the information which was the point of the lesson?

If you are concentrating on a lot of the details above, it becomes hard to keep it all in your head, particularly if you are changing classes, so it is worth keeping a notepad handy to make notes of things which look helpful for the future, e.g. behaviour management techniques or methods of teaching. You can't have too many of either.

Most teachers are happy about this but if the teacher looks dismayed about you taking notes in his/her lesson, smile and say something like, 'Thank you for that. I've picked up a few tips and jotted them down.' Try to look eager and non-judgemental. Don't look like an inspector.

Other things to do
Most of these can apply to either primary or secondary school.

- Sit in on as many different age lessons as you can to get a wide picture.
- If you are in the school on the first day of term in September, try to find an experienced teacher who will allow you to sit in on his/her first lesson with a new class. The first contact lesson is the most important lesson of the week because the teacher establishes the foundation of his/her relationship with the new class. Some teachers like this time alone with a new class, but if you can sit in on one, you might learn something about establishing a positive relationship.
- Try to spend some time in youngest and oldest classes, to give you an idea of the range of the school.
- Go to assembly every day because they vary enormously even within one school. It lets you see what appeals to children and it might give you some ideas.
- Offer to help with marking of the class lesson you have just observed, because it gives you a better view of the range of children's ability. If the teacher doesn't want an unqualified person marking his/her books, ask if you can just look at them to get an idea of what the pupils can do.
- If you are in the same class for a few sessions and are feeling confident, you may ask the teacher if you could take part or all of a lesson, or help a group of less able pupils.
- Ask if you can sit in on their planning meeting.
- Offer to hear the children read, or read a story to the class (primary). You can learn a lot by observing, but there is nothing like practical experience to learn to do the job properly.
- Have a look at the National Curriculum documents for your subject (secondary) or age range (primary). It's never too soon to start accumulating information.

This should be a stimulating week for you. Hopefully it will give you ideas for the age range you want to teach and the type of teacher you want to be.

When you start college

When you start college you will probably be given an opportunity to discuss the placement with lecturers and other students and be given some follow-up focused tasks to get you to think about what you learned during the placement. For example, one task might be directed at ensuring that you are familiar with the transition period before pupils come to secondary school. It will be easier to relate to them if you know where they are coming from.

You may be asked what you have learnt from your visit and what benefit it was to you. You will be asked to describe how things were done in the class (or classes) and analyse how effective it was. How you describe and comment on the effectiveness of the teachers you observed and how efficiently the school provided for the pupils' needs will give your lecturers a fair idea of how well you are engaging in finding out about the complexities of the job. Try to keep at the front of your mind that during this discussion the lecturer is trying to find out about you, not the school.

Early on in the course you may have an assignment about pre-course placement as part of your professional studies course, e.g. you might be asked to explain the system set up for dealing with children with special needs, and discuss its effectiveness.

3 Getting through the Course

PART 1: IN COLLEGE

Freshers' Week

This term is used for the first week at any college or university whether it is for teacher training or another degree. If you have left school within the previous year, Freshers' Week can be a stimulating experience. You can finally throw off the 'school kid' image and step into the adult world.

For 18-year-old students who have left home for the first time, there might be a mixture of enthusiasm and nervous anticipation. Some may be trying to hide their homesickness. Those who arrive at a college from overseas and do not know anyone can find it nerve-wracking to find themselves suddenly alone and away from home.

For the younger students, the first priority is to get to know the other students to make friends. These are the people who will support and encourage you through the pressure of exams, writing essays and dissertations and teaching practice. Do not underestimate their importance. Young people feeling unsure of themselves are sometimes tempted to try to impress their peers. This often antagonizes others who are not feeling confident and the facade falls apart quickly. You will make friends more quickly and keep them if you avoid putting on an act.

What goes on?

There will be a week of activities to help you familiarize yourself with the university, its routines and find out who everyone is. It is a quick way to widen your circle of acquaintances and make friends.

Most students and lecturers to whom I spoke gave the following advice.

- It is best to attend every event whether it is compulsory or not.
- Disregard any predetermined ideas given to you by others and go with an open mind.
- Students' clubs and societies vary from the highly intellectual to the trivial; from the politics and debating societies with their prestigious speakers to the Winnie-the-Pooh society. There will also be lots of different sports clubs, musical and dramatic societies, religious and cultural organizations. There is bound to be something of interest for you.
- Make sure you join a few clubs to help you get into the swing of things, meet people and make friends. If you are shy of going alone at first, persuade someone to come with you. Other students may be only too glad of your company.
- This is also a time to learn about yourself. You may find all sorts of new things which interest you, and find that you have talents of which you were unaware.

The following advice is from students who have completed the PGCE or GTTP courses.

- Be willing to immerse yourself in the course for the duration. If you are married make sure your partner knows that you will not always be available to support him/her for the time of the course.
- Have an escape activity if you can. Preferably something which is completely unrelated to the course.
- Some students on one-year courses told me the trainees had widely varying attitudes. There may be some who are not taking it seriously and who will deliberately or inadvertently bring others down with them by depressing them with negative attitudes or trying to distract them from their work by suggesting something more interesting to do than go to lectures. Don't let them wreck your chances. Give them a wide berth.

Lectures

Lectures take different forms. Sometimes there are a hundred or more students in a lecture theatre and you are not allowed to ask questions unless invited. So instead make a practice of taking notes and jotting down questions to ask in your seminar group or tutorial group.

In others there is more interaction between the lecturer and students. Although it is tempting to sit in lectures just soaking up all the information and taking notes, it is also wise to ask questions when you can, to get the best out of them. It is exactly the same as the school classroom situation.

Most students told me the best lectures are the ones which are geared up to what you are about to do, e.g. lectures on teaching practice just before you do it to give you ideas, or on subjects which you have chosen for an essay or assignment. Others said they gained a lot from the lectures which came after the placement because the theory had turned to practice and now made sense to them.

Lectures where there is interaction between the lecturer and students or students and other students and active participation by students are most productive.

Some students find the lectures interesting and helpful. Some find a high correlation between the theory and the practice while others complain that they are a waste of time because they only want to get out into the schools and start teaching.

The content of the lecture may seem too far removed from your immediate needs but remember it is a long time before you retire and information and ideas flowing today may well come in useful one day.

You must always remember there are many ways to do everything and lecturers are giving you suggestions which will work with all classes some of the time and some classes all of the time. Don't fall into the trap of thinking that anything works with all classes all of the time. You will eventually need to experiment and find out which methods you find easiest to use and develop the skill of finding new methods for yourself.

Everyone accepts that the experience in the school far outweighs the value of the theory, but don't underestimate the theory. Knowledge is power and you can't have too much of it.

Being organized

Remember that your information is only useful when it is readily accessible. Keep your notes carefully because the subject of a lecture may come up in the classroom several months later when you thought you had forgotten it. It is time-economic to invest in sets of file dividers for your ring-binders and arch-lever folders with the contents of each section clearly marked and your pages numbered. The small amount of time spent on it at the beginning can save you a lot of time later on when you need information quickly. Lecturers say that students waste a lot of time through being disorganized. Remember lost time means added stress.

How to get the most value out of lectures

It is surprising how much agreement there was between lecturers and students to whom I spoke about this. Here is a précis of what they said:

- Always approach lectures with an open mind. Don't allow yourself to be thrown by new ideas. Be willing to try out new things in the classroom.
- Lecturers with long years of experience have ideas and beliefs of their own. You can accept their ideals or reject them as you wish, but only after you have thought about them, not before.
- Try not to switch off, even if you do not agree or feel bored or tired. Engage with lecturers, for if you don't you will probably grow into the type of teacher who cannot engage with the pupils.
- Few lecturers, if any, profess to know it all. Most accept that there are many ways to teach and learn. They are unlikely to object to your questioning their ideas and suggestions and frequently welcome students with an enquiring mind. So don't be afraid to speak up and debate with them.
- In lectures avoid sitting near those who are not interested and want to have their own little chat to pass the time. That means sitting near the front for they will be at the back.
- If you can't avoid them, feel free to ask them to save their chat for later as they are spoiling the lecture for those of you who are interested and do want to learn. Students are often wary of speaking out, afraid that they will be accused of being 'swots',

but other students who are also irritated by them will thank
you for it and probably admire you for shutting them up.

- Asking questions during lectures when it is allowed helps you
to get the more out of them. It is a similar situation to the
pupils in the classroom: they learn more when they are
actively involved.

- If you do not feel confident enough to speak up in a lecture,
you might instead discuss the subject with other students to
see if they agree with you. Don't worry if you cannot quickly
draw conclusions about what works best. It takes discussion
and experience to decide what methods work best for you.

Essays

Many students dislike writing essays because they find it tedious and
too far removed from the practice of the classroom. Eager for
hands-on experience, they complain that writing essays is a waste
of time. Don't get caught out with that attitude. To the experienced
teacher or lecturer it sounds arrogant. The old maxim – what you
put in is what you get out of it – applies here.

There are usually lots of essays to write covering a range of
topics, about which you might in some cases have a choice. Some
are subject-based and some are related to issues which arise in
school such as bullying. Other popular topics are inclusion in education, differentiation, behaviour management and assessment policies. Essays on any of these topics can be specific to individual
academic subjects.

This is an opportunity for you to do your own research in the
library and read various papers on the topic to draw conclusions and
form opinions of your own. Although it may seem like pure theory
when you are writing the essay, it gives you a chance to find out
about best practice and refine your ideas.

Some students complain that it is a waste of time but it is important to think long-term. The information may not be useful immediately but during the years which follow you will find that the job
is so long, wide and varied that you cannot have too much information. In fact I have known advisory teachers to say that when
you think you know it all, it is time to give up because you are
clearly past it.

Tips on essay writing
- Always choose a topic which interests you.
- Look closely at the list of Professional Standards for QTS. Is there a topic which you could study to show that you are aware of and understand all the implications of it? Try examining all of the subsections of Section Two – Knowledge and Understanding. There are lots of possibilities there to demonstrate your awareness of educational issues and hopefully fulfil the criteria of the standards as well.
- Avoid 'essay crisis' at all costs. Start reading as soon as you can after receiving the question. A last minute job is never your best.
- Read a lot of literature before you begin writing because different books, DfES documents and educational newspapers and magazines will give you different angles from which to look at issues including ones which you have not thought of. Make a lot of notes.
- Talk informally to other people about the essay topic. Your peers, your lecturers, teachers whom you know, even your children if they are at school and it is a relevant topic. Everyone has a viewpoint and discussing issues sparks off ideas which you would otherwise have missed.
- Remember that before professional writers start writing they spend a lot of time thinking about it. After they have written it, they will probably leave it for a few days and go back to it to improve it. The same rules should apply to you writing your essay.
- The Internet is useful, but never adequate on its own.
- Rather than piling up a mountain of notes, try using a dictating machine and just speak into it. It is much faster than writing or typing unless you are a competent typist.
- One student told me how she recorded some lectures on a mini tape recorder. A useful extra if your budget can stretch to it.
- Go through your written notes with a highlighter and mark what is relevant to your essay topic. This should cut down your notes quite drastically.
- Similarly listen to your tape and make notes of the points which are relevant.
- Study the brief or question closely to make sure you have answered the question.

- Being concise is better than a lot of extra words.
- Take essay deadlines seriously and deliver it on time to avoid that feeling of irritation when it is returned to you with the words 'LATE' in red letters on the front, when you have missed the deadline by minutes.

Assignments and Projects

Assignments and projects are specific tasks to make practical investigations in order to find information. They are different from essays (and, I always found, more interesting) because as well as the background reading and making notes, you also have to carry out a test or experiment, make observations and/or record results, analyse the results and draw conclusions, which have to be presented with careful and reasoned argument or explanation.

How are they helpful to the student?

Carrying out assignments involves more active learning than writing essays and so many students find it more beneficial. Having to draw your own conclusions based on information which you have found out for yourself helps you to formulate your own ideas with more confidence, than merely accepting what you have read in a book.

Some assignments are time-consuming and so are not practical to carry out when you have a full-time teaching job. This is an opportunity to find out things which you will not have time to investigate in the future.

Most assignments are school based and concerned with looking at practice in the context of an authentic classroom. Students have the opportunity to find information about issues like assessment, behaviour management, how pupils learn and how teachers can engage their interest.

As with the essays, you can kill two birds with one stone by looking at your list of Professional Standards for QTS and finding topics which will fulfil the criteria for some of them. Before choosing a subject, always check the document to see if you can find an interesting subject which will fulfil one from the list.

Lecturers tell me they make the activity useful to students by giving lots of constructive feedback. Where students make large errors of judgement it is important to help them onto the right lines as early as possible. Try to see assignments as a long-term benefit. As with everything else you do at college each item is likely to be of benefit some day.

Examples of assignments and projects
These vary in both subject and method. The following are examples given to me by recent students.

1. Observational assignments
One student told me of an assignment 'To examine teachers' interactions with pupils to find if there is a gender bias'. Some students observed teachers working and made tally charts of the interaction between female pupils and teachers, and male pupils and teachers, whether it was initiated by the teacher or the pupil or whether it was negative or positive.

At the end of five or six lessons some found around a startling 80 per cent of the interactions of both male and female teachers were with boys. It is important to learn from findings such as this that some members of the class take up a disproportionate amount of the teachers' time, and so put you on guard against falling into a trap such as neglecting the girls.

Some students' findings and conclusions could of course be different from that of other students. When carrying out this type of assignment it is important when stating your conclusions to add a sentence or two acknowledging that your experiment/investigation was on a very small scale and so cannot always be taken as representing the school population as a whole.

2. To examine the range of ability within one age group
Another type of assignment is when students are asked to carry out the same set of activities with a bright pupil, a moderately able one and one of lower ability of the same age group. At the end you might see a staggeringly wide gulf between the lower end and the top end of the ability range in the class.

From this you will learn the value of providing different levels of work for the different ability groups within the class. Many teachers see this as a reason to retain grammar schools.

It might also make you aware that putting pupils into streamed classes for some subjects makes it easier to give pupils more attention because the teacher is not being stretched in all directions at once. You might also become aware of the value of providing a support teacher for less able pupils to work in a small group to help them to keep up with the class.

3. Finding ways of developing good practice

Another example might be to write a set of lesson plans for your main subject, make resources, deliver the lessons and evaluate them. When teaching a topic, e.g. electricity, find out what difficulties the pupils have and how you could help to resolve them. What every-day activities can you devise to make the lesson more interesting for them and how would you improve it in the future? How can you make the topic relevant to their everyday life?

From this you learn that even the best prepared lessons can go wrong and even the lessons which go well can be improved. The important part will be finding ways of preventing difficulties which you had not previously anticipated and thinking up interesting activities to make the lessons exciting.

This is an invaluable activity because it is what you will need to do when you are qualified and your colleagues and pupils will appreciate you being able to do it well.

4. Focusing on developing skills across the curriculum

Some assignments are longer and students are given a topic to research over several weeks to find information and use it to produce a body of information and ideas, e.g. find ways in which pupils' learning can be improved by using ICT, or how to make lessons accessible to children who are in the early stages of learning English, or have special needs.

This of course requires observation of teachers demonstrating good practice and discussion with specialist teachers. Don't be afraid to pick their brains. You will also need to find opportunities to try out methods and see what works best for you.

Most students to whom I spoke found these 'hands-on' parts of the course interesting and helpful. Most emphasized the importance of only choosing topics which were of most interest to themselves.

Mock-up Lessons in College

A mock-up lesson is one where students take turns in preparing a lesson to deliver to other students who role-play as pupils. Some students find this a nightmare in their first year of college. The confident and the extroverted find it enjoyable. Once you get used to it you will probably find it helpful.

The advantages of mock-up lessons include:

- If you are feeling nervous about taking your first lessons they are an opportunity to have some practice before being faced with the 'real thing'.
- You are forced to focus your mind on how to explain things clearly and lucidly so that pupils can understand.
- You get instant feedback from the lecturer and other students.
- In some colleges the lesson is videoed and played back giving students the opportunity to view their own performance, make a self assessment and listen to constructive suggestions for improvement.

Disadvantages are:

- Some students find them daunting, even terrifying.
- They are not authentic. You are not actually having to take responsibility for the management of equipment and the pupils' safety and behaviour.
- They force students to focus on themselves as performers instead of the pupils as learners, but class teaching is also about management of groups of learners; matching work to pupils' abilities, managing resources and groups who can work in harmony. Even if you shine in the mock-up lesson, it is still possible to find the real thing difficult.

Coping with the banter

In my college, the exercise was civilized as long as the 'class' was all female but if it was a mixed group it occasionally turned into a farce. It was seen as a golden opportunity for students to poke 'innocent' fun at each other. It only needs someone to keep interrupting with silly questions, or saying 'I don't understand' to everything and constantly asking for a repeat explanation to spoil the whole exercise.

On primary courses, it has been known for male students to crawl along the floor looking up a female student's skirt and interrupt with dopey remarks like, 'Hey Miss, I can see a hole in your knickers'. If this happens to you it's best to ignore it or laugh and continue. Don't let it sting your pride or attempt to sort him out in a teacherish way. The offender will only have a ball winding you up for the rest of the lesson.

If the ribbing continues the best response is to adopt a Joyce Grenville tone and say, 'Now Jimmy, do up your flies and stop playing with yourself. That's a good boy.'

Mock-up lessons are worst in the PE hall, where safety rules are so strict. When a student role-plays the naughty child by climbing up the apparatus before it has been checked, try saying, Joyce Grenville mode, 'Now children, stay away from the wall bars. I'm hoping Jimmy will fall off and break his neck.'

If you cannot cope with all this ribbing, give up now, or restrict yourself to applying for jobs in very civilized schools.

It's all different in the classroom
When you find yourself faced with a lot of cheeky half-heard remarks in a real classroom, it is a fine art to know when to ignore silly comments and when to stamp on them firmly. It obviously matters less during the mock-up lesson in college, but when you get into school, it is important to stamp on the comment which is causing definite disruption and spoiling a lesson.

However there will be times when the pupil is deliberately trying to wind you up and you will find it more effective to pointedly ignore him/her while giving a lot of very positive, kind-natured attention to others. You will only get this right every time after you have got to know a class.

Exams

Exams are most important for the B.Ed. student because the results decide what class of degree you get, whereas your teaching practice will only be classified as a pass or fail. Some students complain that this system is so heavily biased towards the academic, since your ability to write essays does not always reflect your ability to relate well to pupils, manage their behaviour and facilitate their learning.

This system could make it tempting to do only the bare minimum necessary to pass your teaching practice but it is better to think long-term because the more effort you put into your teaching practice the easier it will be to cope with your induction year.

PART 2: TEACHING PRACTICE

The Preparation

Teaching practice (TP) is the most stimulating and productive part of teacher training. In some colleges students, quite profitably, spend much more time in school than in college. It is also the part which gives you the clearest idea of how much you like the job and how well you can cope with it.

Although the class of your degree may be decided by your academic performance, making a success of teaching practices is also vital to passing the course. I have been told by lecturers that if they are uncertain whether to pass a student they use the yardstick of whether they would want the student teaching their own son or daughter. A valid way to decide!

I have known many student teachers who have entered schools nervously for their first teaching practice, and emerged at the end of it with renewed confidence. It is also the part of the course which causes a lot of students to have second thoughts. Many who drop out of the course do so after a bad experience of teaching practice.

One problem is that students come across irritations and difficulties which they have not anticipated. Sometimes this means having to do extra TP during the college holidays, because they did not perform well enough or had time off when they found it stressful.

Some found nits in their hair, or had a miserable time after inadvertently offending the head or a class teacher. Some students find it more difficult than being a class teacher because working within someone else's framework can be so much more restrictive than creating your own.

Although many teachers are helpful and supportive towards students, a small number are unsympathetic and find them a nuisance because they create extra work and may accept a lower standard of work and behaviour than the class teacher, who then has the task of pulling the standard back up when the student leaves. Others take advantage of students and leave them to cope alone while they take unscheduled non-contact time.

I have known students to give up after working with unhelpful class teachers or heads of department on teaching practice while others, determined to cope, rose above it and emerged stronger.

Many of the pitfalls could have been avoided with a little prior thought.

Protect yourself as well as the pupils

1. Know the basic rules

In almost every school, there is a rule banning everyone from leaving children unsupervised by an adult. This is because they are not insured if they have an accident, and parents can sue for compensation. It's never worth taking the risk of leaving pupils alone, especially as it is more difficult for unions to defend you if you have broken the rules.

2. Join a union or association

It is wise to join the students' section of a teachers' union or professional association. If you are left in charge of pupils and one has an accident, or worse, makes an accusation against you, it is reassuring to know that legal advice is at the end of a telephone. Also, if the worst happens and a parent tries to prosecute you, there would be legal backing to prepare your case and defend you in court. Be sure to check before you join, that the above service is included.

One lecturer told me that her college actually calls in union representatives to advise students before they go to schools. If you are fortunate to be in a college which provides this service, attending the meetings with the union reps is essential.

Usually membership is free to students and some teachers' unions and associations even give a reduced fee membership when you start your induction year. Often students join several different organizations. In case your college does not provide you with the information, a list of unions and professional associations is in Appendix 2 at the back of this book.

3. Accusations and allegations

In today's unhappy climate of child abuse, teachers are sometimes suspended if a child makes an accusation against them, until an investigation by the police has taken place. The same can apply to students on teaching practice.

Although it is rare for teachers to be charged, any teacher who has been wrongly accused has found the weeks of waiting an unbearable strain, and some have given up teaching because of it. Because it is so easy for children to make accusations, many heads and teachers advocate that you never allow yourself to be alone with a child. Accusations against teachers and students are hardly likely to succeed where there are witnesses to refute them.

In the past, an adult's word was always considered more reliable than a child's. Now the balance has shifted, so it is sensible never to allow yourself to be in such a vulnerable position.

4. The 'touching' question

Many members of the profession advise teachers never to touch a child, because it can be misinterpreted as an assault. This is easier in a secondary school but in an infant school, small children often want their shoelaces tied, cut knees wiped or a cuddle when they fall and hurt themselves. Unjust as it may seem, statistically, men are more at risk than women.

It is wise to leave the First Aid to the school's staff designated for the purpose, only tie up shoelaces and buttons in front of witnesses and unless you know the parents well, never risk giving a distressed child a cuddle. If a child wants to cuddle you, it's often all right to accept it, as long as you do not initiate it or respond to it. If you find it uncomfortable, you can smile and say gently, 'That's very nice, but I don't need a cuddle just now.'

All of this amazes teachers from abroad and those who left school more than twenty years ago. It is a sad reflection on our society, that teachers are shown so little trust and minors are given so much power without responsibility. If found to be lying, pupils, even over the age of 10, are not prosecuted for wasting police time, as an adult would be.

In these litigation-happy days, as long as teachers and others working with children are in such a vulnerable position, we are stuck with having to take so many steps to protect ourselves.

Relationships with other trainees

Teaching practice can be a lonely business if you find yourself in a school with no other students. Usually there is at least one other student. It is vital that the students give each other morale support.

This is no time to be competitive. When people at work start competing they stop cooperating: and schools run most efficiently on a basis of unity and team work. The same principle applies to students. Sharing and supporting are the keywords. You can discuss your lessons together, offer suggestions and be ready to encourage each other. Tell each other what is going well for you and what mistakes you have made so that they do not fall into the same trap.

Different Formats of Teaching Practice

Teaching practice takes a variety of forms depending on the college or university and whether it is a four-year B.Ed. course or a one-year PGCE.

Teaching practice is tiring but you will benefit by being better prepared for your induction year. There will be a sudden rise in your workload. Sometimes students find themselves spending one hour preparing for a one-hour lesson. This is obviously unsustainable in the long term but in the short term it may be necessary. Try not to look on it as time wasted because the better you are prepared the better your lesson will be and the experience and any resources you have prepared for it are things which you will take away with you and use in the future.

The B.Ed. course

In some of the B.Ed. courses, you can be sent to a school for about four to six weeks or longer as the years progress. In a primary school the weeks will be divided into two so that you can spend about half in two different classes, usually a Key Stage 1 class and a Key Stage 2 class. This is useful because it gives you a modicum of experience of both and helps you make up your mind in which you want to specialize.

A few of the difficulties to be overcome

In a B.Ed. course, the teaching practices are shorter and although this means it is not so tiring, it also means that it is harder to make your mark in a school because you have only just got to know the place by the time the practice is over. Also the children know that you are only there for a short period of time. In some schools this makes little difference, but in a school which has suffered high turnovers of staff, it is harder to get the pupils to take you seriously, when they know you are here today and gone next month.

Different schools have a different ethos. Anything which is valued in one school may be given little attention in another and so you have to be flexible and ready to adjust to the school. Remember that no school is ever going to adjust to a student.

Getting acceptance from teachers is important. Some don't want to be bothered and so it is you who has to make the extra effort to get on with them in order to get help from them.

The days when teachers routinely gave students a free hand to try out anything they wished are long gone. The NC has imposed a stringent workload on schools and so they are bound to insist that students follow the school's programme. It is probable that you will have to follow their syllabus for the whole practice. They may even have the lessons planned out to the last letter and give you no flexibility. If you want to change this, you will have to wait until you are reasonably well accepted and the alternative that you come up with will have to be at least as good as the lessons they have planned.

Some teachers do not want to let go of their form and hand over to a student. This is not just possessiveness. Students sometimes let a class get out of control and the standards slip. As it becomes clear to them that you can cope, they will gradually trust you more and give you more responsibility and the more conscientiously and competently you work, the more licence you will have.

Students often dislike the teacher who tries to strait-jacket them into doing everything exactly the way they would do it themselves. They feel they are being cloned. If you find yourself in this position, it is best to accept it for the first week or two and then say something tactful like, 'It's been great having you give me the lesson plans to make it easier for me but I feel I must try to do more for myself rather than lean on your expertise all the time. Would it be all right if I planned the next lesson and if you think it's OK, try it out?'

It might be irritating if they refuse but you will have to keep it at the back of your mind that the school is doing you and your college a favour and so you must not mess it up either for yourself or students in the future.

Post-graduate courses

In some post-graduate courses you can start by going to a school for two days per week and college three days during the first term. It is great to get down to the job quickly with hands-on experience because there is a lot to learn in less than a year. However some students have told me that it was difficult to keep their university work and their school work going at the same time. Also, after they took lessons for two days they had to return to college and so they lost the continuity of the scheme of work. Students also find it difficult to establish a working relationship with pupils and teachers on this part-time basis.

Although this is difficult to get used to, it is important to remember that this will only last a short time, and when you qualify the problem will disappear and so it is best not to let it worry you now.

As the PGCE year progresses you will be sent to other schools for up to about ten weeks full-time during which you will have to cope with about 60 per cent of a regular teacher's timetable and so you will find this more satisfying as you will have the opportunity to build up relationships with pupils and staff and hopefully see progress, which is so satisfying.

Easing Yourself into the School

This is not advice on the technicalities of organizing a successful lesson. You will receive plenty of that from your lecturers. The following points can apply to anyone.

Which school?

Some lecturers have told me that their colleges are conscientious about matching students to the school where they can do the work which interests them most.

For a successful teaching practice it is essential for students to work harmoniously with their mentor in school. Over a space of time, lecturers build up relationships with the mentors in schools and try to put students into schools where they will have a mentor with whom they can work harmoniously. This of course is the ideal, but even with the best will in the world, it is impossible for this to be successful in every case because it may not be so easy in a college where the staff have not had the chance to build up enough contacts or become familiar with the staff of all the schools with which they work.

A FEW TIPS

- If you have any choice, never go on a teaching practice in a school where a member of your family works. If you make a mess of something, you don't want to fight the flak on the home front as well as work. College lecturers are usually sympathetic about organizing this.
- If you are allowed any say in where you go, find out from friends and any teachers you know in the town which schools are reasonably civilized.
- Before you ask for any particular school, look around the area first.
- Look at the school's website for information about the school and in particular look up www.ofsted.gov.uk to read their last inspection report and check their place in the league tables. The more you know about the school the better.
- If you have any definite needs like children of your own at school, impress on the lecturers early the need to be in a school close to home. Most are accommodating about this.

Coping with a range of people

Personnel skills are important for teachers and students. Everyone in the school must work in a mutually supportive manner. You are unlikely to succeed unless you can work comfortably with the full range of people.

The points below should help you to deal with each one.

1. The class teacher/head of department

Within the school the class teacher (primary) or head of department (secondary) are the people on whom you are most dependent and they are the ones who write the report on your performance.

- Try to stay on the right side of the class teacher or head of department. Stay cheerful and offer to help them with extra tasks in the class or department. They can make your job much easier or more difficult.
- Find out what time your class teacher arrives and try to be in the classroom at the same time or earlier. It is easier for a teacher to be positive towards you when you show you are keen.
- Always ask about anything you don't know. No one will think you foolish; in fact they will like your willingness to learn.
- If you find yourself working with a teacher or head of department who is unhelpful, make sure that your college supervisor is aware of it.
- If the teacher keeps wandering off and leaving you to cope alone, try not to complain unless it is a very challenging school because it might make you look weak. If you can cope alone, think of it as an advantage because it will give you confidence. Sometimes it is easier to cope without the scrutiny of a teacher's critical eye. Remember that class teachers can not write a negative report on you if they haven't seen your faux pas. If you really cannot manage, just ask the teacher to stay in for the whole of the lesson.
- If the class teacher/head of department tries to press extra responsibilities onto you, tread carefully. If you don't think you can cope, say something tactful like, 'I don't think I can manage that on my own, but I don't mind giving you a hand with it.'
- If a parents' evening takes place while you are there, ask the teacher with whom you have the best relationship if you can sit in on the interviews. They may not allow you, but if they do, it is a useful opportunity to pick up a few tips on how to carry out this tricky part of the job.
- If an Ofsted inspection is imminent, the teachers will be so taken up with the pre-Ofsted frenzy that they will not have much time for you, so you must make sure your college supervisor is aware of it.

2. The pupils
- Before you go in, ask the teacher or head of department to explain the discipline strategies used. If you are left alone with

a class that is difficult to control, it makes it easier to cope if you use the system to which the children are already accustomed. Consistency is the keyword.

- Ask the teacher if there are any pupils' personal circumstances you should know about, e.g. bereavement in the home, parents separating.
- Get a friend to go through your hair to check for nits. If you catch them they can be removed with a fine tooth napp comb or ask at the chemist for the shampoo for the purpose. In fact get a napp comb anyway because during recent decades, there have been epidemics of nits. This is not just a problem in impoverished inner-city schools: it can happen anywhere. If you have long hair, they are more easily avoided by wearing it up.
- Be wary of the advice about stimulating the pupils all the time. It makes them hyper-excited. Always throw in a peaceful lesson per day.

3. Your college supervisor
- Always make your supervisors welcome when they come in to observe your lesson. They are human too and you need to keep them on your side.
- If you have the dilemma of your college giving you a list of tasks which the class teacher/head of department refuses to allow you to carry out, it is wiser to accommodate the teacher, who has the power to insist anyway. Explain to your supervisor that you were afraid to press the issue, in case it spoiled the college's relationship with the school. I have known students, who tried to solve the problem the other way round, and the most miserable weeks of their college careers ensued.
- When your college supervisor gives a demonstration lesson, remember to say that it was interesting/stimulating/achieved its objective.

WHAT YOU CAN EXPECT OF YOUR COLLEGE SUPERVISOR
Your supervisor is there to support you if you feel you are not getting adequate support in school. Some students have been in schools where they were given the worst classes, probably because the over-pressured teachers saw their presence as an opportunity for

them to have a break. If you find yourself in this position tell your supervisor at once. They may be able to persuade the head or head of department to give you a more reasonable timetable.

Supervisors must also keep a close check on the quality of your lessons. Whether your observed lesson goes well or not, it is important to listen carefully to the detailed feedback. If you are told that some part is not adequate, ask for practical guidance to improve it. Remember that it is their job to support and guide you.

Also they can help you accomplish the long, scary list of professional standards. When you meet them, show them which you believe you have achieved and ask their advice on which standard to try next and any suggestions for ways of trying to achieve it.

4. Your mentor

Your mentor is a teacher in the school who is there to guide, support and advise you throughout the teaching practice. For you s/he is probably the most important person in the school so it is vital to cultivate a positive relationship with him/her. In a primary school, your mentor may be one of the class teachers in whose class you are working; in a secondary school it may be the head of department.

Many mentors are excellent, on top of the job, ten steps ahead of you and can give you exactly the right pointers to put you right and give you reassurance when things do not go well. Others are under so much pressure from inside and outside the school that the student on teaching practice is a low priority.

Their first impressions of you in the first two or three weeks will be the ones which will stick and be hardest to change. Throwing yourself into the job right from the start will definitely work to your advantage.

You also need to bear in mind that no two schools are exactly alike and the ethos of one can be totally different from another even if they are in the same neighbourhood. Your mentor is there to tell you what is accepted practice and what is frowned upon.

It will be easier to start off on the right foot if you ask your mentor about the following.

1.   *The behaviour policy.* Discipline is so much easier if everyone in the school is following the same code of practice.

2. *Books, stock, equipment procedure.* Practical everyday issues like whether you can help yourself in the stockroom or is there a book to sign and a list of goods to be recorded. Ask to see what equipment is available for your subject(s) and where it is kept. If the stockrooms are kept locked, only senior staff allowed in and stock is dispensed once a day/week then tread carefully, because this is often a sign that the staff are shown little trust.

3. *Being there.* Find out if you are expected to attend staff meetings and make a note of the dates in your diary because it's embarrassing if you miss them. You will probably be expected to attend school assemblies. You should go to them all because the staff are normally expected to attend, and it irritates them if you are seen to be skiving. It is also an opportunity to pick up a few ideas for the future.

4. *Staffroom customs.* Find out whom you have to pay for tea, coffee and lunches, and pay up front. In a few schools teachers are quick to notice things like this. I once worked in a school where you were allowed a full cup or half a mug of coffee, not a full mug; and another where you were not allowed a teabag to yourself, you had to share with a colleague.

5. *The staff dress code.* It causes resentment if you do not adhere to it.

The rest of the staff

- Offer to do playtime duties. That will balance out a few faux pas.
- If there is an educational or fund-raising event in an evening or at a weekend, it is worth your while turning up to help. That will obliterate all your faux pas.
- If you take pride in your honest, forthright manner of speaking, curb your style for a few weeks. I have known students to have a miserable teaching practice after irritating everyone by giving them the benefit of their advice on how to improve the school.
- Never allow yourself to be drawn into the staffroom politics. It takes longer than the duration of a teaching practice to work out the structure of it, and it's never worth the grief.
- If your mentor or another teacher invites you to join the staff in the pub it is well worth going because it helps to build up

a relationship with them and it all makes it easier to get the wheels turning.

Staying sane

- When you feel like giving up, remember the teaching practice is temporary and you are there to learn for your *own* benefit. Remind yourself that it will be completely different when you have your own class(es), and keep going.
- Stay in close touch with friends from college. You can all share your troubles and comfort each other.
- If you are allowed a few days off for illness during teaching practice, do try to resist the temptation to take a sickie if things become difficult. Remember you might actually be ill later on, and end up having to do extra teaching practice during college holidays, if you have had too much time off.
- You will be amazed how time-consuming the work is, but try to find a period in the week to do something entirely different. A change is as beneficial as a rest.
- If you are cooped up in a centrally-heated building all day, it is worthwhile taking a walk outside at playtime or lunch time to get some fresh air. It is time well spent as it makes you more alert in class.
- Eat a nutritious lunch and try to find a period at lunch time when you can sit quietly on your own and unwind if you have had a stressful morning. It enhances your performance in the afternoon.
- Teaching practice is tiring. You may find you need extra sleep. Worse – you will probably have to curb your social life. Many students resent this but it is worth it for a few weeks and much better than failing and having to do an extra placement.
- When the practice is over, round up a bunch of friends and go out for the night to celebrate or drown your sorrows. It won't improve your grade or report, but it will cheer you up if things have gone wrong.

When you are starting to find your feet

The importance of feedback

After the first few weeks ask your mentor for feedback if you have not already had it. Ask him/her to be specific about what you should focus on to come up to standard. Tell them 'I want to improve on these things so that when I want to apply for a job, I can't be told that I was not up to standard.' Make it clear that you are eager to get things right as you will need all the skills next year.

You need to make the effort to make your mentor work with you. Honesty is very important in your relationship with your mentor. If you are not doing what you are meant to be doing it is important that s/he keeps you informed. It is also important that your mentor gives you the hard facts when necessary. Make it clear that you need the absolute truth from them even if it is negative.

Monitoring your own progress

At your weekly meeting with your mentor, as with your college supervisor, it is sensible to bring your list of professional standards, which you will have received from your lecturers. This list looks quite daunting at first as there are so many targets that you have to achieve.

Show them which you believe you have achieved in the previous week and ask them to sign your file if they agree. Ask their advice on which you should try next and how you might go about it. There are so many to get through it is important to try a couple each week as it could be hard going if you leave them all to the end. See Part 3 of this chapter on professional standards for suggestions.

If you are on a post-graduate course, at the end of the first term ask again if your improvement has been enough to bring you up to standard and do the same after the first few weeks and the end of term in your second school. Unless they have given you specific issues over which you are underachieving, it is difficult for them to fail you.

Getting the support you need

If the mentor is not giving you the support you need then this really must be tackled – with the mentor him/herself in the first instance. It is unfair to go to the coordinator of the mentors before speaking to the mentor first. If this does not work then speak to the coordinator, then your college supervisor if that does not work. At all costs avoid confrontation and do not antagonize them: it is they who will pass or fail you and they have the biggest input into judging your ability to be a teacher. Try a line like, 'I know you have a lot on at the moment but I would be really grateful if you could help me/ give me some guidance on . . .'

When you finally apply for a job the head will seek a reference from him/her, so on your final placement it is especially important to build up a successful relationship.

And now to the Business of the Job

Getting ready to teach lessons

Before you have to do any teaching yourself you will have an opportunity to sit in a classroom to observe the teacher and get the feel of the class. It may also be an opportunity to collect information for carrying out some assignments.

Always keep a notepad handy to jot down anything which you might find useful for the future.

It is worth taking the following precautions to smooth the way.

1. Establish the ground rules

Before you go in, chat to the teacher about what, how and where they want you to be. Some are very easygoing and allow you complete freedom to wander around the room, look at children's books and join in helping them with the work set. Some will even say that you are welcome to chip in and add anything you wish, if it is a subject at which you are proficient.

However even experienced and successful teachers are self-conscious about being observed and may prefer you to sit silently and unobtrusively at the back. Therefore it is important to get things clear to avoid causing difficulties later.

2. It is too soon to be assertive!

It is important to go along with the teachers' wishes at least until they get used to you. If a conflict arises, remember that in all probability the head will back the teacher against you.

3. Beginning to establish a relationship with the pupils

When the teacher allows you to get involved, you can start asking the pupils what they are doing and show them that, although the class is under the control of the teacher, you are eager to be involved as well, and let them see that you are interested in their work. You can start by asking questions to test their understanding of the work or asking a question designed to extend what they have learnt. Let them see that you can teach them. If they feel they can learn from you they will give you more attention than if you have sat on the sidelines, in their eyes doing nothing.

Don't be afraid of questions about being a student teacher. It doesn't matter if they know you are not yet qualified. Children and teenagers are quite nosy. They will probably ask you about your accent and where you come from if it is different from theirs.

However some might start asking how old you are and have you got a girlfriend/boyfriend. These can be fended of politely with an answer like, 'Oh that's my little secret'. It's never wise to get too pally. They expect teachers to be teachers, not one of their mates.

Observing lessons

Observing lessons has a twofold purpose.

1. *To carry out assignments.* The dynamics of the classroom is a complex business. There are many things happening in the classroom, which an untrained eye will not spot. Students are given a series of tasks focusing on different themes such as relationships between pupils and teacher, behaviour management techniques or styles of teaching.

2. *To learn as much as you can about controlling pupils, and stimulating them to learn.* Look at the following issues:
   - The use of questioning:
     - What sorts of questions does the teacher ask?
     - Can questions be answered with a simple yes or no, or do the pupils have to give an explanation?
     - Does s/he just ask for information or does s/he stimulate the pupils' thinking?
     - Do the questions test understanding?
     - Are the questions random or are they structured to become a little bit more complicated each time?
     - How does s/he distribute questions?
   - The organizing and managing of a vast amount of equipment for a practical subject like art or science.
   - Organizing and coping with large classes, when the lesson

involves a lot of pupils moving round the classroom and using a lot of equipment to carry out a variety of tasks.

- Provision for a wide range of abilities.
- Techniques for managing pupils' behaviour.

If all of the above are too much to take in at once, at the beginning just concentrate on one of these issues per lesson.

Lecturers say that the students are given a variety of observation tasks, one at a time, so that they can build up an increasingly wide view of classroom practice. As the days progress, you will find yourself trying to carry an ever-increasing load of information in your head, so it is important to make the load lighter for yourself by carrying a pen and notepad.

Alternatively, if you had a very confident teacher to observe, you could ask if you could video a lesson. You might be lucky and be allowed to do so.

Learning how to deliver lessons

When the assignments are finished, you then have to learn to deliver lessons satisfactorily. It is important to be aware of the objective of each lesson and understand how the lesson is structured to achieve it. Always ask the teacher for a lesson plan, so that you can follow it as it progresses.

Many lessons are in three parts with a warm-up, main part and plenary to pull the main parts of the lesson together and test if the objective has been achieved. Watch how one part of the lesson flows into the next part.

The quality of teaching and learning

Look out for these points. They help you decide what creates a successful lesson and give you an idea of the type of teacher you want to become.

- Does the teacher state the objective at the beginning and make sure the children understand it?
- Are the pupils interested and enjoying their work; are they on task and involved in the learning activities?
- How is the lesson organized – is the teacher doing all the work and the pupils sitting passively, are they working

independently or in groups cooperatively? Or is there a mixture of these?

- Does the teacher do all the telling and explaining or are the pupils given tasks which guide them to find things out for themselves?
- Which of the above do they do most willingly? Which is most productive?
- How does the teacher coax the less interested pupils to take part?
- How does the teacher deal with the pupil who is hell-bent on disrupting the lesson?
- Is there much interaction between the teacher and pupils, pupils and other pupils? What effect does this interaction have on learning?
- Does the teacher return to the objective of the lesson to check if s/he has achieved it! Have the pupils grasped the concept or developed the skill or do they understand the information which was the point of the lesson?
- At the end do the pupils look as if they have gained some knowledge, skill or satisfaction from it or been bored and irritated by it?

As well as concentrating on how the teacher delivers the lesson you might like to consider some of the issues below. There are too many suggestions to consider in one go. You might choose one at a time. Remember that keeping pupils under control, interested and learning satisfactorily is a complex business, which takes time to perfect. You cannot expect to get it all right at first.

The hidden curriculum

The hidden curriculum is not to be found in any NC document but many teachers, like myself, believe it is central to the success of every school. It is the set of rules of behaviour by which the staff and pupils conduct themselves. Qualities of kindness, honesty, respect for other people, property and authority all set the tone of the school and are the foundation of a happy, successful school, where pupils want to attend and teachers want to work.

I have always found that the general ethos of a school, the behaviour and interpersonal relationships of the staff and pupils, reflect the personality of the head. Those heads who treat the staff even-handedly and with appreciation, tend to have a staffroom full of people who extend the same goodwill to their colleagues and pupils.

You can get a fair idea of the school's hidden curriculum by observing these points.

- Is the atmosphere calm, strained, pressurized, happy, hostile? Is there a sense of well-being?
- What does the teacher do to influence the atmosphere?
- Listen to the classroom noise. Is it a hum of activity caused by positive effort to accomplish a task? Is it an argumentative, aggressive noise directing pupils' attention away from their work?
- How would you describe the teacher/pupil relationship? Is it friendly, respectful, cooperative, antagonistic, hostile?
- Is the classroom a pleasant environment for teaching and learning? Do the wall displays contain interesting examples of children's work. Are they informative, attractive, inspiring, boring, faded from being there too long or falling off the walls?

Behaviour management

Behaviour management of pupils is crucial to delivering the curriculum successfully, keeping the pupils on board and preserving the teachers' sanity.

Depending on how the pupils are normally managed and the level of support that the parents give to the teachers, it can be an easy, straightforward task or a horrendously difficult one. These points give a few clues as to how it is done.

- How long does it take the class to settle down after break-times or first thing in the morning? A minute, five minutes, ten minutes?
- How much time is wasted through the pupils coming in late, teacher arriving late, resources not being readily to hand, mis-behaviour of pupils or conflict between pupils or teacher and pupils?
- How does s/he control the pupils? Does the teacher instil fear, use incentives, rewards, punishments, or a mixture of some of these, and which does s/he use most?

- How does the teacher deal with difficulties? Does s/he antici-
  pate them and prevent them happening?
- Does classroom layout play a part in managing behaviour?
- Does the teacher's relationship with the pupils play any part
  in how well s/he controls them?
- Do the pupils automatically give their allegiance to the
  teacher or does it have to be earned?

Establishing satisfactory behaviour management

If everyone in the school has difficulty with a particular class then
that is not a suitable class for the novice teacher. Sometimes teachers, exhausted by disruptive classes, see the student as a resource to
give them a break. You could diplomatically ask your mentor or
your supervisor to support you by asking that you be given a
different class. Don't worry that you might look weak. Their job is
to give you positive experiences from which you can learn. They
must ensure that students do not have to cope with too much too
soon so that they give up and the profession loses them.

If you cannot escape from having to take the ultra-challenging
class, at least don't demoralize yourself by thinking their behaviour
is your fault. Comfort yourself with the thought that teaching practice is short and you will then escape.

Behaviour management can be made easy for you from the start
if the regular class teacher is in the classroom with you to back you
up. Also, pupils are less likely to misbehave if their teacher is watching. But of course eventually you will have to learn to cope alone.

Establishing a positive relationship with pupils is the foundation
of effective behaviour management. If you start off well the rest falls
into place more easily. If you and the pupils rub each other up the
wrong way on the first lesson, it can take a long time to mend the
situation, probably longer than the duration of your placement.

Most of the following tips can apply to either primary or
secondary.

- Learn pupils' names as quickly as you can and try to pronounce non-British names correctly. It is easier to get their
  attention if you address them correctly.
- Start each lesson on time; set the tone that they have to
  be present and prepared at the start of each lesson. This is

especially important in secondary schools where pupils are changing class and have every opportunity to be late.

- Speak respectfully to pupils. You will only get respect if you give it out.
- Use a quiet, firm, polite manner to lay down your parameters before you start.
- As far as possible use the same discipline strategies for incentives and rewards as their regular teacher. The pupils respond better when the routine is clear and consistent.
- Make it clear in advance what you want pupils to bring to each lesson.
- If you know in advance that a pupil is likely to be tricky, it is a good idea to ask a teacher who teaches him/her what works best.
- Alternately, catch him/her out doing the *right* thing. When they are doing what you want, say, 'That's cool, Simena'. It is so much more effective than rebuking them for doing the wrong thing.
- Establish a clear, simple routine to your lessons at the beginning. When you are feeling more confident that your pupils are under your control you can try more adventurous lessons.
- Always prepare much more work than they can handle. The devil soon finds work for idle pupils.

The 'don't' list

- Never actually lose your temper. If you lose control of yourself, you have almost certainly lost control of them. In the more challenging schools pupils love to see a teacher losing it while they sit back and grin. You can, of course, have a controlled loss of temper, i.e. just pretend to have lost it. It can work if you do it on rare occasions only.
- Never back a child into a corner from which they cannot escape, otherwise they will come out fighting. Try to always give them an opportunity to get out of a tight corner and conform.
- Never keep on repeating the same punishments which are clearly not working, If a sanction (or a reward) does not work after two or three attempts, try something different.

- When pupils threaten to bring their parents to the school to sort you out on their behalf, don't look dismayed. Lift your diary and say, 'That's great, I was hoping to meet them, I'm free this afternoon, bring them in.' I have never known a parent to turn up after that.
- Try not to shout at pupils for misbehaviour. (Well, hardly ever.) Noisy teachers have noisy classes. It has more effect the less often you do it.
- Never shout to attract attention from a noisy class.
- Try not to automatically blame the pupil. S/he may well be at fault, but sometimes pupils are insecure in the presence of new teachers, particularly if they have an unstable home. It may be that they are preoccupied with home problems and your lesson is the least of their worries. Don't be afraid to ask your mentor or a class teacher for advice. They know the pupils and their background and the reasons for their behaviour and often a few quiet tips can reduce the problem.
- If a child is cheeky and you respond in the manner of a teacher who has been there for twenty years – the 'I have never in all my life heard such nonsense . . .' sort of comment – the children will know you are bluffing and it will make them eager to expose you. Try 'I used to try that one with students when I was at school. It didn't work then and it won't work now.'
- Never try to be one of the lads/gals. It will backfire because they will not take you seriously as a teacher.
- Never let your exasperation show. Save that for your mentor or other students in the staffroom.
- Never imagine that you know it all. I have been teaching for over 30 years and am still learning new strategies. If you make mistakes be prepared to learn from them.

The 'do' list

- Try to stick to the school behaviour policy as consistently as you can. Pupils like to know where they stand.
- Always give a clear explanation if there is a change of procedure. No one likes to be confused.

- Listen to pupils. They love it, especially the worst behaved. Often they don't have enough opportunity for conversation at home.
- Have a system for attracting everyone's attention. Some infant teachers rattle a tambourine. For older children, I always say, 'Hands up those who are listening,' and follow it up by adding, 'Good, Abdul, you can go out at playtime,' to whoever's hand goes up first. In a secondary school, raise your voice a little and say, 'Quiet please. Quiet everyone. Third time, quiet!' Another effective approach is always to establish the practice of releasing first, at the end of the session, the pupils who were all giving their attention first.
- When a child is messing about when they should be working, start with, 'Can you manage? Would you like some help?' Not 'Stop talking/stop messing about/don't be so lazy'.
- When you get comments like, 'I'm not doing this, I don't want to,' smile sweetly and say, 'No problem, you can do it at lunch time.' Or 'That's fine. You can take it home and do it. I'll speak to your parents and tell them. They won't mind', whichever works best with the individual child. This often works, especially after you have carried it out a time or two.
- Remember, pupils who don't respond to threats and sanctions often respond to praise. Use lots of it on disruptive pupils, when you can.
- Give positive instructions: 'Please work quietly,' not, 'Stop making that din.' Or 'Write slowly and carefully to keep it neat,' not, 'Stop rushing through it and making a scruffy mess.'
- Before imposing a sanction, give pupils a clear chance to conform. You might say, 'Your behaviour is not acceptable, you have got from now to lunch time to get yourself back on track or your lunch break will be spent in here working with me.' Or establish a practice of three strikes and you're out, i.e. each time you give a warning remind the pupil that if s/he has to be warned twice/once more s/he will be in detention, lose break-time or whatever is the normal practice.
- Always try to impose sanctions the same day if at all possible. They lose their effectiveness if they drag into the next day.

- Once you have made the threat and the pupil is determined not to conform, make sure you carry it out. They will never take you seriously again if you don't.
- Seating arrangements can alter pupils' behaviour. Seating boys beside girls sometimes calms either one of them down, or hard-working pupils beside those not so desperate to learn.
- Try to come across as one who is there to help them and so it becomes unreasonable for them to try to undermine you.
- Keep the praise flowing, but not so much that you devalue it.
- Ask another teacher if you can observe them working with the class so that you can see how they manage the behaviour. Observation is one of the best ways of learning.
- Keep notes about any serious incidents in case there is any problem with parents later.
- If a pupil is cheeky, never ignore it or give the pupil the satisfaction of seeing that it winds you up. You might reply, coldly but calmly, 'Rudeness will never get you anywhere with me. If you do not know how to speak to other people politely I can keep you here at break-time and teach you.'

Other adults in the classroom

It's not enough to sort out the curriculum and the pupils. As the job has become more complex and the demands of it increase annually it has become the accepted practice to have more adults, qualified and unqualified, in the classroom. A few teachers prefer to work solo, but many are efficient at using the help of others to benefit the pupils. Consider the following.

- What other adults are working in the classroom – classroom assistant, parent volunteer, support teacher, advisory teacher?
- What are their roles and how do they contribute to the children's learning?
- Do the other adults work in isolation with their own little group at an activity which is different from the rest of the class; do their pupils take part in the same lesson as the class with the help of the adult; does the other adult share the lesson delivery equally with the class teacher?
- What is the difference in the role of a qualified person and an unqualified person, e.g. a parent volunteer.

When you have observed several teachers, you might like to reflect on these points.

- Does the 'hidden curriculum' vary from one class to another?
- Do the teachers all manage their children's behaviour in the same way? How do they vary? Do different techniques provide different types of behaviour?
- What causes the difference in their methods? Is it the age of the pupils, the number of disruptive pupils in the class or the teachers' personality, or a mixture of both?
- Do all teachers treat their support staff the same or differently?
- Which teaching styles inspire the pupils best and least?
- How does the atmosphere of the classroom affect the quality of learning?

Observing the points above should give you ideas about how you want to organize your lessons when you start teaching.

It is a tall order to get all of the above issues absolutely right in every lesson. It's a bit like driving a car. An experienced, competent driver makes the task look easy. Similarly with teaching, it takes a lot of practice to get to the stage of making a complicated lesson look easy.

Also remember that the process of getting everything right is a never-ending journey. After thirty-something years at the chalk-face, I am still learning new tricks of behaviour management and providing more interesting ways of engaging pupils in active learning. Don't let difficulties get you down or failed lessons dishearten you. See them as an opportunity to learn something new and improve your performance.

As with the pre-course placement it is worth taking the time to jot down notes on anything you see that might be useful for the future.

Styles of teaching
In the beginning, with unfamiliar pupils you might like to copy the regular teacher until you find your feet. This is fine for feeling your way in gently and safely. The teacher will appreciate your compliance with his/her advice. When you have gained some confidence, then is the time to experiment. Ultimately you will develop your own style for there is no need to be a clone of someone else.

On teaching practice don't be afraid to experiment. If things go wrong it doesn't really matter because no one is expecting you to get everything right. On the first teaching practice you might be team teaching with another PGCE student or class teacher. This makes it easier if the lesson needs a lot of organizing.

Don't be afraid to experiment and take a few risks. This is an opportunity to find out what works and what doesn't. Students and teachers who have never had a failed lesson have probably never tried to do anything more exciting than the bog-standard. Even if the lesson collapses you will probably learn something from it. Teachers and lecturers should be sympathetic as long as you have put effort into the planning and made a conscientious attempt to get things right.

The following suggestions can be adapted to either primary or secondary.

Variety is the spice of life – Routine in our lives is useful to let us all know where we are going, but with teaching it is important to vary the activities because it all becomes very humdrum and unstimulating if there is no element of surprise.

Keeping their attention – It is tempting to imagine that because they are sitting quietly looking at you that means they are taking in all you say, but frequently pupils realize that if they sit quietly and say nothing you will do all the work while they mentally go to sleep. This is talking *at* pupils and must be avoided because most of what you are saying is going over their heads. Remember that they have limited concentration, like all of us, and their attention will wander if you do not make sure you are talking *to* them and they are engaging with you.

Use questions to keep everyone's attention –

- If you need to give a long or complicated explanation, you can stop every three or four sentences to ask a question to maintain their attention. To engage them all in the answering ask 'Will the bulb in this circuit light up? Hands up those who say yes. Hands up those who say no. Hands up those who don't know.' Then ask a pupil to explain why or why not.
- Give out small whiteboards and dry-wipe markers, or scrap paper, at the beginning. When you ask a question, ask the pupils to write the answer on the whiteboard and hold it

up – like naming the Weakest Link. They usually like it and it forces them all to participate. (This applies particularly to primary classrooms.)

- Engage them in the active learning. If a question needs a complicated answer, ask the pupils to turn to their neighbour and take turns in explaining it, before asking someone to explain to the class.

Working in companionship is more fun

Let them occasionally carry out tasks in pairs. Worksheets can look so tedious to work on, on your own. Let them occasionally do them with a partner. They spark ideas off each other and the companionship encourages them. It often works well if one is a little more able than the other, but of course you must not allow the most and least able to work together because they often irritate each other as one soon gets left behind. However it is not advisable to do it all the time as they need to be able to work independently as well.

Interactive whiteboards

An interactive whiteboard or smart board is a computer operated screen that allows you to interact with the computer. It has a special surface with a laser attachment that enables you to interact with the software by moving images and captions on the board.

In some schools everyone has one and in others they have yet to be introduced. They are a boon to the modern teacher. Pupils love them and so you can add a creative touch to your lessons. Of course you must save all the information in a well organized system to save time in the future.

Drama to involve all

This works well in lessons across the curriculum. Each of the following ideas can be adapted depending on what topic you are studying and can be used in primary or secondary. It is best to build up a relationship with the class before trying it because control is important during these lessons.

Discussion groups

History. Put pupils into groups of four, two to be Anglo-Saxons and two to be twenty-first century people. Each group has to prepare a dialogue where they explain their own system of law and order to the other and then discuss the merits of each. Each group then presents their prepared dialogue to the rest of the class.

English. Look at whatever book you are reading at the time and select an issue which causes conflict among the characters. For example, if reading Anne Fine's book *The Chicken Gave It to Me*, the pupils can discuss the issue of putting chickens in overcrowded, confined spaces to maximize egg production, against the merits of keeping a smaller number in the open air. Or if reading Captain Marryat's book *The Children of the New Forest*, the pupils can divide up into Cavaliers and Roundheads to discuss the merits of their side in the struggle of the Civil War.

If reading *King Lear*, the pupils could get into opposing groups, to debate whether the king was an innocent victim or deserved his fate by provoking his daughters into rebellion by his obvious bias for Cordelia. The pupils can have an open class discussion or go into groups to discuss the matter and present their dialogue to the class.

Modern languages. Put pupils in small groups to prepare a short conversation using whatever set of vocabulary they are learning at the time, e.g. a chat about holidays, exams, football, any sport or topical subject.

Collaborative activities – finding out for yourself

Working in mixed ability groups on an activity is a great way to learn because children give each other ideas, show each other how to find out things and learn the invaluable skill of working cooperatively. This style of teaching often involves pupils finding out things for themselves.

You must always make sure you have an able child in each group, to organize the others, and if there is a pupil who is in the early stages of learning English try to have another in the group who can interpret. Make it clear that the children with special needs must be included. These ideas can be adapted to whatever you are studying.

Geography. Look at the country you are studying, e.g. Egypt. Give each group a blank map of the world, of Africa and Egypt, and one or two atlases. Give them a list of things to find in the atlases and mark on the maps.

Science. Science lessons at all levels involve group investigations. Even Key Stage 1 pupils can take part in simple finding out activities.

In pairs, give pupils a piece of insulated wire, a battery and a bulb and tell them to try and find out how to make the bulb light. Or give them a few magnets and a piece of paper marked 'Magnetic' or 'Not magnetic' and tell them to go round the classroom to find out and record things which fall into each category. Pupils are stimulated by this because it gives them responsibility, and the pleasure of having found out things for themselves is wonderful.

Maths. Brainteasers – they make a great mental and oral starter for a lesson for pupils to work out in groups. You can get them from http://www.nrich.com.

Maths crosswords work well in pairs or small groups and children love maths games. The catalogues usually have a range of games which teach children a skill and add an element of fun to your lessons.

Preparation

Start small. Don't try to achieve too much in the first few lessons and concentrate on quality rather than packing in lots of activities. Write your lesson plan and then ask the teacher to check it. Remember that it is important to take the children's pace of learning into consideration and the teacher can advise you on that.

Having your lesson observed

This can be nerve-wracking at first, but try to see it as an opportunity to learn.

The acid test of whether a lesson was successful is whether the objective was achieved. You may not always get a warning about when the lecturer is coming so it is best not to be caught out skimping the preparation.

Be clear in your mind exactly which points you are trying to teach; write the objective on the board and start by making sure the pupils know what it means. Finish the lesson by asking questions to test whether you have succeeded, and if so, tell the pupils they have achieved their objective, and add a few words of appreciation.

HINTS TO GET THROUGH LESSON OBSERVATIONS

If there is to be a support teacher in the room, such as a special educational needs or English as additional language teacher, discuss together in advance what you would like them to do and give them your lesson plan as well.

If there is a disruptive child in the class try to place the pupil in the group with the support teacher who is more familiar to him or her. If you have made a conscious effort to build up a comfortable working relationship with all staff with whom you have to work, they will be more inclined to help you in circumstances like these.

- Always make sure you have a detailed lesson plan ready for the supervisor because, if the lesson fails, at least it shows you put time and care into it, and so it won't look so bad.
- Don't worry if you have collywobbles, because most students do, and they usually disappear as soon as you become engrossed in the lesson. It's all right if a lecturer realizes you are nervous because they were once students too.
- If it is a difficult class, tell the college supervisor in advance what the problems are.
- Don't worry if the lesson does fail absolutely: it has happened to everyone.

GUIDANCE FROM THE OBSERVER

Make sure the person who observed your lesson gives you detailed feedback. This has the dual purpose of reassuring you about the things which went well and helping you to rectify anything which went wrong.

Don't take a defensive attitude. Be willing to learn from the feedback because it is designed to help you in the future. If something was poor, ask the supervisor for ideas on how to improve it for the future. Remember, the supervisor is not an inspector: they are there to support you and help you to develop your expertise.

Being a Reflective Practitioner

This is an essential part of the course and a vital element of being an effective teacher. Students who are eager and ambitious often feel disproportionally dismayed when a lesson unexpectedly turns into a mess. If or when this happens to you, there is no need to let it cloud your horizon for long. No student to my knowledge has ever got through college without an occasional fracas and you should see it as an opportunity to learn, not as a failure on your part.

Writing the evaluations to your lessons forces you to think about how to improve them for the future.

Whether the lesson has been observed or not, ask yourself what things went well and make a list of them. Perhaps a few of the pupils acquired the concept or enjoyed it. Maybe the first part went well and then it fell apart when the activity changed. Keep the successful part at the front of your mind before you start analysing why the lesson was not as successful as you had hoped.

What can go wrong
- The resources were not properly organized or there were not enough of them.
- The work was not pitched at the right level, i.e. too hard or too easy.
- You were not absolutely sure of all your information.
- The lesson was not interesting enough.
- The pupils spent too much of the time passively listening and not enough time actively participating.
- You ran out of things to do ten minutes before the end of the lesson.
- You were nervous and the pupils realized it.
- You rubbed them up the wrong way by acting over-confidently or coming over too heavy too quickly.
- Your behaviour management was not adequate.
- There was a bunch of awkward pupils who didn't want to work and their main aim was to prevent anyone else working or wreck the class whatever you did.
- The pupils have had so many student teachers and supply teachers that they are no longer interested in listening to outsiders.

Always make a note on the lesson plan to help you get it clear in your head so that you do not repeat the errors. The following points might help.

The lesson plan and resources
- Preparation of resources is essential. If you have a lot of them, with worksheets at differentiated levels, a simple precaution is to have post-it labels stuck on the top copies, to

avoid the mayhem which arises from pupils getting the wrong one.

- Always have extra worksheets available, one for yourself, one for anyone observing your lesson, a couple for the children who mess it up and one for your file.
- Always have your lesson plan in your hand. You don't need to memorize it until you are more experienced and confident.
- Prepare an extra activity for each lesson so that you won't run out. It is not a waste of time if it is not used because you can keep it in your file for future reference.
- Getting the lesson pitched at the right level can be difficult for someone who is unfamiliar with the class. Always ask the regular teacher to check your plans and preparation before you take the lesson.
- Variety is the spice of life. The more interesting the lesson the less likely they are to look to their peers for amusement.

Discipline
- It is important to hold your head up, look pupils in the eye and speak confidently, but if you overdo it they will not be fooled, especially at secondary level. Try not to be overbearing and definitely never speak in a cutting or sarcastic manner.
- Ask your mentor if there are any behaviour problems in a class *before* you take the lesson and ask for tips on how to manage. Some classes need to handled firmly right from the first minute. In others you need to start with a joke and a laugh to get them on your side and then clamp down later if necessary.
- Make sure you know the school's sanctions for misbehaviour. It works best if you are all following the same system.

Your frame of mind (more important than you think)
- It is impossible to teach for long at the limits of your own knowledge. If you are asked to teach a lesson on something unfamiliar, it will give you more confidence if you read up about it before you get caught out. The hour of your time the night before the lesson is easier to cope with than the uncomfortable hour of regret the following night.
- If the class gives grief to every teacher, be assured that their behaviour is not your fault. A small minority of classes never

give their respect and allegiance to a teacher until they have
established a relationship, and that can take a month in a
primary school and much longer in a secondary where you
only have pupils for a few lessons per week.

- If you are planning something adventurous and worried that
it might fall apart, it gives you confidence if you also have an
easier activity ready in case it all goes wrong. Double work, I
know, but it can give you double confidence and the planning
can always be kept for the future.

Being a reflective practitioner in the school is so important because
you need to sort out specific problems immediately. In the beginning it is often too complicated to do it alone. Your mentor, your
college supervisor, other teachers and your peers can advise you and
guide you to overcome difficulties and correct mistakes.

When you return to college
It is still important to reflect on the experiences and share ideas with
peers. When students are completely away from the pressures of
marking, collecting resources for the next day's lessons and worrying about how to manage the behaviour of the next day's classes,
it is easier to assess the positive and negative parts objectively. It is
reassuring to realize that others encountered similar challenges.
Successful colleges recognize the need for evaluation and give students opportunities to discuss with their peers and lecturers what
works well and what must be avoided at all costs.

It is often quite productive for students to bring resources they
have used or made to group discussion meetings so as to share their
ideas. Teachers do this informally in group staff meetings and
INSET meetings. Occasionally teachers become precious about
their ideas and resources and do not want to share them. This is
poor practice. In the best schools, teachers work in a team, sup-
portively and cooperatively, sharing their skills, using their talents
to encourage others and taking pride in playing their part in helping
others to improve. Foolish teachers become resentful if others copy
their ideas. Sensible teachers take it as a compliment.

It is also important to remember that some methods and practices work well with some classes and can be disastrous with others,
e.g. depending on how they have been trained in the past, some

pupils are able to accept more responsibilities for themselves and can be trusted to carry out investigative tasks sensibly, or conduct themselves around the school unsupervised. Others would see this as a godsent opportunity to go for a smoke in the toilets. The practice must be suitable for the pupils as well as achieving the objective.

If you found some of the placement heavy going it is reassuring to discover that others had a similar experience. Most students find that the chance to talk to other students about what was successful is a valuable opportunity to pick up ideas and console each other.

When you qualify

Being a reflective practitioner is not just for teaching practice. It is an essential element of being a teacher and it is sensible to cultivate the habit of mentally evaluating each lesson, right from the start. Of course, when you take up an appointment you do not have to write a detailed evaluation of every lesson, but it is good practice to make a mental note of anything that worked well or didn't. A quick phrase or sentence on the lesson plan to remind you when you do the lesson next year should be enough.

Coping with Ofsted while on Teaching Practice

'Ofsted' is an acronym for 'Office for Standards in Education'. It sends its inspectors to schools to examine every aspect of school life from the quality of lessons, efficiency of management and budgeting to the cleanliness of the toilets. The last point is not a cynical joke. Some inspectors have been known to check the toilets every morning and tell the head that the cleanliness and suitable supply of tissues and soap were evidence of care for the children.

At the time of writing, a missive from Ofsted announcing the arrival of its staff usually results in feverish activity by the head and teachers to ensure that all paperwork is up-to-date, the school looks stunningly attractive, the most imaginative and enjoyable lessons are prepared, the pupils are interested and on task, the objectives of the NC are being achieved, the parents are satisfied, and a host of other issues.

At the moment (2005) Ofsted are piloting a practice of cutting the notice period down drastically. Whatever the timing and format of inspections in the future, they are likely to continue to generate anxiety and a degree of ill-feeling throughout the profession.

A small number of students have to cope with Ofsted while on teaching practice. If you find yourself in this unholy position you might like to consider the following advice.

The 'do' list

- Go to your mentor if you are nervous and ask if it is absolutely necessary for you to be inspected. If it is your first teaching practice, you have more chance of avoiding it, but if you are nearly qualified, less so.
- Tell your college supervisor that you are under more pressure because of it.
- Think positively. If your lessons are judged to be satisfactory or better, it will look impressive on your letter of application for your first post.
- Keep at the front of your mind the fact that you will not be there to pick up the pieces when the event is over.
- Ask your family or flatmates not to expect much sense out of you until the wretched inspection is over.
- Forget the social life until it is over. You can make up for it when it is over.
- Make sure that every detail of your next day's lessons is prepared before you leave each day.
- Get a proper night's sleep.
- Eat properly and stop for a rest at break-times.
- Stay close by any other students who are in the school. You all need each other for support and encouragement.
- Forget anything that anyone has done to annoy you during the preceding weeks. You still have to work together and that can only be achieved in an atmosphere of harmony.

The 'don't' list

- Don't panic. This tends to reduce the quality of performance.
- Don't expect the school staff to be their usual cheerful selves. Their careers are much more affected by the inspection than yours and arguments over petty issues sometimes arise when people are under pressure.

- Don't go off 'sick'. This destroys your credibility as others always suspect absentees of malingering. You will get more sympathy and kudos for turning up even if your lessons are not brilliant.

Parents' Consultation Evenings

These are sometimes called Open Evenings. Conducting a parents' consultation evening in a confident, efficient manner is a necessary part of the job, if you are to maintain your professional credibility. Teachers get little training for it and many newly qualified teachers face their first parents' evening with trepidation.

You can learn a lot from observing how teachers conduct the interviews, so if a parents' evening occurs while you are on teaching practice it is sensible to ask if you can sit in on the interviews with a teacher to pick up some hints on how to conduct them. Some teachers may veto your presence, but you may be fortunate and find a teacher who welcomes your company.

Sitting in on a teacher's interview

The following points can apply to primary or secondary. Some teachers are so expert at handling tricky situations that they make the job look easy. In time you will see that keeping the parents' support makes your job easier too.

You might want to write down a few details afterwards but obviously not in front of the parents as that could be quite disconcerting for them and perhaps make them clam up. Of course if the parents are being rude or aggressive it might just make them calm down.

Points to note when you sit in on a parents' evening with the class teacher in control.

- How does the teacher greet the parents?
- How does s/he make them feel at ease?
- What vocabulary does s/he use to break news of poor exam results, or examples of misbehaviour?
- How does s/he use different tones of voice?
- How does she cope with parents who are distressed by their children's behaviour or poor performance?
- How does s/he diffuse a heated situation?

In case you have to do it alone

As a student you will probably not have to cope with a parents' evening on your own, unless you are doing a long placement in a secondary school and you are the person who has had most contact with the class in your subject in the preceding weeks or months.

Parents' evenings are tiring after a long day at work, but if you do take part in one the experience will give you some confidence for when you have to do it on your own next year. The suggestions below are for students who find themselves facing parents alone.

KNOW THE SCORE

Even in very civilized schools there can be parents who view the open evening as an opportunity to attack the school in general and the teacher in particular. As a precaution you could take your class list(s) to a teacher who is familiar with the parents and ask him/her to give you a brief rundown of the list to tell you which may be difficult and how best to handle the situation if it becomes tricky. Of course you must make a few notes because it is hard to keep it all in your head when you are also trying to recall so many details about the children as well.

If you are in a challenging school ask if there are any parents with whom it is unwise to be alone, in which case you might like to ask a senior member of staff to accompany you or at least patrol the corridor outside your classroom while you leave the door open.

There may be parents who are over-punitive with their children and it is important to know this in case a pupil suffers an over harsh punishment because of something you said.

The last two points are not an exaggeration. I have encountered both on more than one occasion.

LOOK AND FEEL RIGHT

Never start an interview immediately after the pupils go home. Give yourself time to have a cup of tea and a snack, freshen up your face, comb your hair, even change your shirt/blouse before the first parent(s) arrives. Remember the type of parent who comes to scrutinize teachers will be doubly keen to size you up if they know you are a student. If you look and feel fresh, you will perform better.

BE PREPARED

It is too difficult to keep all the information in your head. Make brief notes on each child. They don't have to be detailed as only you will see them. It is irritating afterwards to remember something you forget to say.

PRIVACY IS PARAMOUNT

It is important that all details remain strictly private; therefore only have one child's parents in the room at any one time unless it is a large room and you can ensure there will be enough space between those you are interviewing and those waiting.

KEEP THE ATMOSPHERE CALM

Sometimes parents are nervous before interviews with teachers. As soon as the parents walk through the door, stand up, smile and say 'Good evening', and introduce yourself. Whatever the quality of your relationship with the pupil, it is best to start by saying something positive about him/her.

MAKE SURE YOU ARE THE ONE IN CONTROL

Always make sure you are the one to start the dialogue. If you intend to say anything negative, have the pupil's books ready to hand in case the parent argues.

It is more persuasive to make your comments in the form of a fact rather than an opinion. It's better to say, 'I have seen your son deliberately distract other pupils during lessons', rather than 'Your son is badly behaved during lessons'. Similarly, 'Your daughter often arrives late for lessons/regularly leaves her homework at home', rather than 'Your daughter is lazy/careless/indifferent'. Facts are more difficult to dispute than opinions, and giving specific examples adds weight to your comments.

If you know in advance that you will have to say something negative ask other teachers if they have the same problem with the pupil. If so, ask their permission to say that his/her behaviour is the same in their classes. It is more difficult to argue if two or three teachers say the same thing.

USE HONEY NOT VINEGAR

Remember, criticizing a pupil can be hitting a parent where it hurts them most, so it pays to be as diplomatic as you can. Saying, 'I like your son, but unfortunately I do find myself having to nag him to stop having private conversations in class because it spoils the lesson for others', is more likely to gain their support and goodwill than, 'I'm sick of your thoughtless son trying to wreck my lessons', even though the latter may be closer to the truth.

DON'T LET A DISAGREEMENT TURN INTO A CONFRONTATION

Most parents approach parents' evening in a spirit of goodwill, but a tiny minority come looking for a confrontation and others become confrontational when they cannot handle a teacher's criticism of their child.

As a student, inexperienced and not yet qualified, you should not have to cope with a confrontation, so you can pass the buck with a clear conscience. If you sense one coming, stop the conversation before it arises, making a comment like, 'I think it would be best if you discussed this matter more fully with the head/head of department. Would you like me ask him/her to make an appointment to see you?'

If parents become aggressive or raise their voices, look them in the eye and say calmly but authoritatively, 'I am not prepared to conduct this interview in an uncivil atmosphere. If you cannot speak politely this interview is now over'. If they do not calm down, stand up and open the door. If they refuse to go, leave the room yourself and go to your mentor/head of department/head to tell them the full facts as soon as you can. They should support you. In fact they ought to feel rather bad about putting you into the situation in the first place.

This type of incident really should not happen but it is important to know what to do if it does.

TRY TO FINISH ON A POSITIVE NOTE

If parents are unhappy at the end of the interview, try to make them feel that you are still interested in their child by saying something like, 'If you are concerned about anything in the future you can make an appointment to come in and see me again. You don't have to wait for another open evening' (unless of course they are the type of parents who want to come and talk to you for an hour after school on a regular basis).

The Post-mortem

Students react differently when the placement is finally finished. Frequently some who started in trepidation return to university with renewed confidence but sadly some who have had an unhappy experience start having second thoughts about whether they want to continue.

Before you make any irrevocable decisions, it is better to give yourself a few days' rest and then try to work out why some of it went pear-shaped. Start by making two lists, one saying what went well and one saying what went wrong.

What went right?

Everybody has some things going well in their teaching practice. Your list might look something like this.

- Some of my lessons went well.
- Some pupils said they enjoyed my lessons.
- I managed to fulfil two or three of my professional standards each week.
- The class that started off being unruly knuckled down and listened to me eventually.
- I kept my file up to date.
- My mentor said my evaluations showed an understanding of the issues.
- I made some worksheets which the teacher said worked well.
- I was able to use a classroom observation or other activity to complete an assignment or essay.

What went wrong?

I have known students to suffer one or more of the points below and come away with a bad taste in their mouth, wondering if they were in the right profession. Your list might look like this.

- The pupils – I could not get on with them or they were so unruly I could not manage them.

- The mentor – s/he did not give me enough support.
- My college supervisor – s/he undermined me more than supported me.
- The head – I fell foul of him/her and s/he made life unpleasant.
- The subject(s) – I did not find it so interesting from the other side of the school desk *or* I did not have enough opportunity to do the things I wanted.
- The staff – they were too busy to welcome me or give me any advice or help *or* I rubbed them up the wrong way and they isolated me.
- The organization and paperwork– it was all too much.
- The journey – it left me too shattered to be at my best.
- Job satisfaction – I suffered as much frustration as satisfaction.

If you're thinking of giving up

First look at your two lists of positive and negative points and it might cheer you up to discover that there were more good points than bad.

Unfortunately, in your mind, one or two bad points can cause you so much grief that they overshadow the positive aspects. It's only when you write them down and compare them that you can see the true balance clearly.

Always remember that both positive and negative points can overspill into other areas of the job and create more problems, e.g. an unsupportive mentor can dishearten you whereas a supportive one can spur you on to succeed.

Look again at your negative points. Now ask yourself how many of them were your fault and could you have behaved differently. The ones which were not your fault will probably not exist in the next placement. If something was your fault, well, don't worry because we have all made mistakes along the way. Whatever mistakes you made, you will certainly not repeat them in your next teaching practice.

It may be that you were just unlucky and things would have been much better in a different school, in which case you should not consider giving up until you have tried another placement because schools vary so much, even within the same area. Another few months and another placement in a different school might completely change the landscape, so try not to give up until you have given it another go.

Also, think about the future. Unless you have something better to which you can move on, you will be back to square one of finding a job or establishing a new career. When you qualify many problems may well disappear when you are employed full-time with a mentor who sees you as a colleague, not as someone who is here for a few weeks and then gone forever.

Getting Organized for the Future

For a teacher, time management is vital. Every lesson represents your valuable time and energy, so you need to develop strategies for conserving both. It is never too soon to take a trip to the stationer's to equip yourself with a set of ring-binders, file dividers, plastic wallets and sticky labels to start collecting your own resources. You may find an online supplier who delivers cheaply in bulk, so you could club together with other students for an order. Buy paper wallets by the gross: you'll be amazed how quickly you fill them up.

As soon as you are certain you are going to stay in teaching, you can invest in a filing cabinet. You don't need a new one, they can be bought cheaply second-hand from office suppliers and sometimes you can be lucky and buy a load of used suspension folders to put in them, but do check the sizes before you buy, because they can vary more than you might think.

Look at all your plans and resources. Divide them into two piles – 'save it and file it', or 'chuck it'. Have a section for each subject and subdivide it for Year groups or Key Stages. There's no need to limit yourself to your own ideas. If you see a useful worksheet or resource made by a teacher or student, ask for a copy. As long as you are willing to share your resources, they won't mind you using theirs. In fact most teachers take the view that imitation is the sincerest form of flattery.

As soon as you have taught a lesson, put a copy of the lesson plan, the worksheet, and any other notes on videos, websites or books and page numbers into a file. Have your files labelled for each subject and divided up for each topic, so that the next time you come to teach it, perhaps in three years' time, you can retrieve the information quickly.

Remember, there is no value in collecting resources if they are kept in a muddle. The time you will lose in searching for them will cancel out the time you have saved in keeping them.

PART 3: PROFESSIONAL STANDARDS FOR QUALIFIED TEACHER STATUS

In order to qualify for QTS it is necessary to fulfil all of the criteria of the Professional Standards. They vary slightly for primary and secondary and are grouped under five headings:

1   Professional values and practice
2   Knowledge and understanding
3.1 Planning, expectations and targets
3.2 Monitoring and assessment
3.3 Teaching and class management

On first looking at this list, you might feel rather daunted at the prospect of having to provide evidence that you can satisfy every single one, but remember many of them are issues which will come up naturally throughout the year. At the time of writing there are about 44 subsections to be fulfilled and the course is about 40 weeks, so if you aim at two per week you will be finished with plenty of time to spare.

Some of the topics would make an interesting subject for an essay, project or assignment, so you could study the essay topics to see which ones coincide with a professional standard and so use it as an opportunity to kill two birds with one stone. When you meet your mentor or personal tutor, it is worth bringing your list and discussing with him/her which ones you want to work on that week and run past them your ideas on how to do it. Once you have established that weekly routine the list will not seem so daunting.

It is important to fulfil as many standards as you can during teaching practice. When you have your weekly meeting with your mentor in school, or your college supervisor, always ask which they feel you have fulfilled and check that they can be signed off; and tell them what your ideas are for trying in the next week. Don't be afraid to ask for suggestions for ones you should attempt next. If you aim to fulfil two or three each week, you should easily be able to work your way through them by the time you reach the end of your last teaching practice.

Remember, some of them are ongoing and so you might have several dates in the column marked 'Opportunities to practise'. At all costs avoid leaving them to the last few weeks as that can result in avoidable stress.

Where the standard requires you to have knowledge or understanding of an issue, it is wise to ask questions about it. Some students fall into the trap of being afraid to ask questions in case it looks as if they don't know enough. This is the wrong attitude partly because it prevents you from learning and partly because teachers and lecturers do not expect students to know everything in any case. They interpret your questioning as evidence of your eagerness to learn, not ignorance of a subject. In fact when students ask advice about how to help pupils they interpret that as a shift in their focus from themselves to the pupils and see it as progress in their growing confidence and professional skill.

As you work your way through them, try to think long-term. Try to keep it at the front of your mind that you are fulfilling the criteria to give you opportunities to learn and become a competent teacher, not just to get through the course.

The following suggests ways in which you could do each one. Of course these are not finite lists, nor could you possibly carry out everything suggested below. For several you may need the regular teacher's permission or support, but they are normally so pleased that you are saving them a job, they are usually only too glad to agree.

Most of the suggestions could apply to either primary or secondary.

1 Professional values and practice
Those awarded Qualified Teacher Status must understand and uphold the professional code of the General Teaching Council for England by demonstrating all of the following.

Standard criteria
1.1 They have high expectations of all pupils; respect their social, cultural, linguistic, religious and ethnic backgrounds; and are committed to raising their educational achievement.

SUGGESTIONS FOR FULFILLING 1.1

- When marking pupils' books start with a general positive comment and then write 'Target:' and add a suggestion which is suitable for that pupil to improve his/her work. One poignant general comment is better than lots of red ink throughout the work.
- Praise pupils generously, particularly the less able.
- Put a Shap multicultural calendar of religious festivals on a class notice-board.
- Point out the festivals as they come round.
- Include a religious festival in your RE lessons (if applicable).
- Put up a multicultural display at an appropriate time.
- Do an assembly to inform about a current festival of another religion.
- Ask pupils to explain to the class how they have celebrated a recent festival, e.g. Eid, Chinese or Jewish new year.
- Try to pronounce their names correctly or at least avoid the temptation to give them a simpler, shortened or Anglicized version of their name. I have known teachers to cause offence unwittingly by doing so.

Standard criteria

1.2 They treat pupils consistently with respect and consideration and are concerned for their development as learners.

SUGGESTIONS FOR FULFILLING 1.2

- In your weekly meeting with your mentor, show your concern for pupils, especially individuals who may need extra support, by mentioning any difficulties which you have had and asking for advice to improve matters.
- Prepare lessons which are interesting and contain simplified activities for the less able and extension work for the brightest.
- Be willing to spend time out of class giving extra help to pupils who need it or request it, or set and mark extra home-work for pupils who are falling behind with their work.
- Keep the praise flowing liberally but not enough to devalue it. Sarcasm is the least effective form of persuasion and inspiration. Make certain that there is no place for it in the classroom.
- Highlight examples of 'good learner' traits as they occur.

Standard criteria

1.3 They demonstrate and promote the positive values and behaviour that they expect from their pupils.

SUGGESTIONS FOR FULFILLING 1.3

- Always be punctual for classes especially after lunch times and playtimes, because it sends out a negative message if you are always the last one into the classroom. Likewise, if you have to collect a class from the playground after each break it promotes a poor attitude if you regularly make a class wait longest in the cold. (primary)
- Try to start classes on time. Don't make the pupils who have arrived punctually wait for the stragglers. (secondary)
- Encourage pupils to take pleasure in each others' achievements.
- Make certain your own manner of address is respectful by giving polite, positive Instructions, i.e. 'Please work quietly so as not to disturb others', not, 'Shut up!' or 'Stop that racket!' (This one can be impossible to adhere to in all cases because most teachers will eventually meet the class which makes a point of trying your patience beyond any human endurance.)
- Don't be aloof. When you meet your pupils in the corridor, smile or nod. If you meet them in the supermarket or the street, look pleased to see them, smile and say 'Good morning'.
- Try to always mark pupils' books before you return them. If they are not marked it looks like you don't consider the work to be important. If ever you don't have the work marked before returning the books, give a reason and an apology and move on swiftly.
- Offer praise and positive reinforcement more liberally than negative. Catch reluctant pupils out doing the *right* thing and praise, ignoring lesser elements of negative behaviour when you can.

Standard criteria

1.4 They can communicate sensitively and effectively with parents and carers, recognizing their roles in pupils' learning, and their rights, responsibilities and interests in this.

SUGGESTIONS FOR FULFILLING 1.4

- Attend parents' evenings if they occur during your teaching practice, even if it is only to sit in during the interview if the teacher does not want you to take part.
- Make a point of stopping to speak in a friendly manner to parents as you chance to meet them.
- Consult parents for support if you think it appropriate but ask the advice of your mentor first.
- Before you speak to a parent ask advice from the regular teacher in cases where the parent is known to be difficult. Inform the parent politely of any problems, making it a request for help rather than a complaint. Try to start the conversation with a positive comment like, 'Jimmy is good at getting on with others and working well in class but I'm finding it hard to get him to bring his homework in on time. I should be really grateful if you could check that he has done it every Tuesday night and put it into his bag'.
- Finish the conversation by telling them they are welcome to contact you if they have any concerns about their child's education. (Of course you should never use this line in a school where parents are pushy, over-anxious or so bored that they want to come and talk to you every day.)
- If there is improvement in the pupil's work or behaviour after you have spoken to the parents, tell them so and thank them for their support because they need to feel appreciated too.

Standard criteria

1.5 They can contribute to, and share responsibly in, the corporate life of the school.

SUGGESTIONS FOR FULFILLING 1.5

- Turn up and help with any fund-raising or pupils' social events like school discos which take place while you are on teaching practice.
- Offer to help with any extra-curricular activities for which you have a skill, like helping backstage for drama productions, Duke of Edinburgh Award Scheme, or accompanying teams on away matches.

- Volunteer to go on school trips, even if they are not one of your classes. (Teachers are always looking for extra support for trips, the experience is beneficial and you will probably enjoy it.)
- Attend any staff social events to which you are invited.
- Offer to take assembly and break duty. You will gain from this too because teachers will appreciate your effort and probably respond by giving you more support, and a better report.

Standard criteria

1.6 They understand the contribution which support staff and other professionals make to teaching and learning.

SUGGESTIONS FOR FULFILLING 1.6

- If you teach science or ICT, make sure you follow the school's procedure for booking resources in plenty of time for the lab technician to organize. (secondary)
- For practical lessons always finish your lesson five or ten minutes early to ensure that the classroom is left tidy and the chairs are up on the tables to make life easy for the cleaners. (Always stay on good terms with the cleaners – you might need to ask them to keep an eye open for small pieces of apparatus which get lost during the day.)
- Even if some support staff like classroom assistants (CAs) are not qualified, they are entitled to the same levels of politeness and kindness as the head and other teachers and probably more than the less benign members of Ofsted. If you set the example, the pupils should follow. If they don't, correct them instantly. It also increases the CA's allegiance to you.
- Always take time to establish a friendly, working relationship with all SEN, EAL, any other support teachers and CAs, over coffee in the staffroom.
- It is good practice to include the support staff in your planning where appropriate, and take time in advance to explain activities in detail to the CAs. Always thank them afterwards as they will always support you more enthusiastically if they know they are valued.
- Ask the teacher if you can sit in on interviews with the Educational Psychologist (EP) and Educational Welfare Officer (EWO) to learn about their roles.

Standard criteria

1.7 They are able to improve their own teaching by evaluating it, learning from the effective practice of others and from evidence. They are motivated and able to take increasing responsibility for their own professional development.

SUGGESTIONS FOR FULFILLING 1.7

- Until you become familiar with a class, show your lesson plans to your mentor/head of department, class teacher, and ask for suggestions to improve them.
- After each lesson write an evaluation on the lesson plan, making at least one suggestion for improving it next time you do it and try to put it into practice as soon as you can.
- Likewise for feedback from lessons that have been observed. Try to use the feedback to improve your next lessons and in your evaluation describe how your change of procedure has improved your lesson.
- After a difficult lesson, chat to other teachers as soon as possible and ask for suggestions on how to avoid similar difficulties in future.
- If you are not snowed under with marking, ask other teachers if you can sit in on their lessons during your non-contact periods, saying what particularly interests you. Experienced teachers do this.
- Even if it is not compulsory ask if you can attend any staff INSET that takes place while you are on teaching practice.
- Carry out lesson observation activities suggested by your college and evaluate what you have learned from it.

Standard criteria

1.8 They are aware of and work within the statutory frameworks relating to teachers' responsibilities.

SUGGESTIONS FOR FULFILLING 1.8

- Read the Bristol Guide 2/95 or 4/94.
- Ask your mentor to clarify any points that you find unclear. (That shows you have a knowledge of it.)

2 Knowledge and understanding

Those awarded QTS must demonstrate all of the following.

Standard criteria

2.1 Have a secure knowledge and understanding of all the subjects they are trained to teach. For those qualifying to teach secondary pupils, this knowledge and understanding should be the standard equivalent to degree level.

SUGGESTIONS FOR FULFILLING 2.1

- For secondary students this point should be fulfilled by having a degree in your subject. Refer to any other relevant qualifications which you possess.
- For both primary and secondary, you can point out that your demonstrating your knowledge and understanding is ongoing throughout your teaching practice.

(For primary teachers who have to teach a wide range of lessons, they may have to take small amounts of extra reading to prepare for individual subjects which were not the subject of their degree, because when teaching a subject you cannot cope by teaching at the limit of your own knowledge.)

Standard criteria

2.1a For the Foundation Stage, they know and understand the aims, principles, six areas of learning and Early Learning Goals described in the QCA/DfES Curriculum Guidance for the Guidance of Foundation Stage and, for Reception children, the frameworks, methods and expectations set out in the Numeracy and Literacy Strategies.

SUGGESTIONS FOR FULFILLING 2.1A

- If you have not studied it at college, borrow the documents above to familiarize yourself with the detail.
- Teach a Literacy and Numeracy Hour lesson every day or most days. (Reception)
- On your lesson plans write in the reference for the objective from the relevant NC document.

- Ask to be involved in the school's assessment and record keeping system for recording the children's progress through the Early Learning Goals.

Standard criteria

2.1b For Key Stage 1 and/or 2, they know and understand the curriculum for each of the NC core subjects, and the frameworks, methods and expectations set out in the National Literacy and Numeracy Strategies. They have a sufficient understanding of a range of work across the following subjects: History or Geography; Physical Education; ICT; Art and Design or Design and Technology; Performing Arts and Religious Education to be able to teach them in the age range for which they are trained, with advice from experienced colleagues where necessary.

SUGGESTIONS FOR FULFILLING 2.1B

- Study the documents for your age range to familiarize yourself with the detail.
- Make sure you teach as many lessons as you can in every subject and evaluate them, including what you would do to improve the lesson if you have to do it again.
- On your lesson plans, write in the reference for the objective from the relevant NC document.
- Chat informally to experienced teachers over coffee. They often have very inventive minds and are full of ideas for teaching mundane subjects in an engaging manner.
- Ask to look at the school's resources and use them. Expanding your knowledge does not involve reinventing the wheel.
- Practise, practise, practise. There is no substitute.

Standard criteria

2.1c For Key Stage 3, they know and understand the relevant NC Programme(s) of Study, and for those qualifying to teach one or more of the core subjects, the relevant frameworks, methods and expectations set out in the National Strategy for Key Stage 3. All those qualifying to teach a subject at Key Stage 3 know and understand the cross-curricular expectations of the NC and are familiar with the guidance set out in the National Strategy for Key Stage 3.

SUGGESTIONS FOR FULFILLING 2.1c
- On your lesson plans write in the reference for the objective from the relevant NC document.
- Ask teachers in the department if there will be any cross-curricular events (e.g. a combined geography and science field trip) and offer to help.

Standard criteria

2.1d For Key Stage 4 and post–16, they are aware of the pathways for progression through the 14–19 phase in school, college and work-based settings. They are familiar with the Key Skills as specified by QCA and the national qualifications framework, and they know the progression within and from their own subject and the range of qualifications to which their subject contributes. They understand how courses are combined in students' curricula.

SUGGESTIONS FOR FULFILLING 2.1d
- Try to attend the meetings for Years 12 and 13, choosing courses so you can be familiar with how A-levels feed into different university courses, e.g. to study medicine, chemistry is the only absolutely necessary subject at most universities.
- Similarly you need to know which GCSEs are necessary for which A-levels, e.g. if you want to study A-level biology, GCSE chemistry is strongly advised: it is important for you to attend any meetings for Year 9 pupils who are choosing their GCSE subjects if they take place during your TP.

Standard criteria

2.2 They know and understand the Values, Aims and Purposes and the General Teaching Requirements set out in the National Curriculum Handbook. As relevant to the age range they are trained to teach, they are familiar with the Programme of Study for Citizenship and the National Curriculum Framework for Personal, Social and Health Education.

SUGGESTIONS FOR FULFILLING 2.2

- Study the NC and the school's own programme of study for Citizenship and PSHE.
- On your lesson plans, write the reference for the objective from the relevant NC document.
- You will probably be limited to teaching their programme but this is to your advantage because you cannot go far wrong if you are following their line.
- Ask if you can observe or take part in any activities on Citizenship or Personal, Social and Health Education.

Standard criteria

2.3.1 They are aware of expectations, typical curricula and teaching arrangements in the Key Stages or phases for the ones before and after the ones they are trained to teach.

SUGGESTIONS FOR FULFILLING 2.3

- If you are in a primary school, ask to spend a session or two in the other Key Stage, if you are not spending any other time in it.
- If you are in a secondary school, recall your pre-course placement in a primary school and say how you valued the opportunity to get a detailed view of the pupils finished off in primary school.
- While on teaching practice, seek a visit to a feeder school, primary or middle.
- Choose an essay or project which requires a visit to another school or Key Stage, e.g. Compare and contrast the teaching of (a topic from your subject) in Key Stage 2 and 3.

Standard criteria

2.4 They are aware how pupils' learning can be affected by their physical, intellectual, linguistic, social, cultural and emotional development.

SUGGESTIONS FOR FULFILLING CRITERIA 2.4

- Look at your choice of essay titles. Is there one on the effect of these background influences on a child's learning. A well thought out essay should ensure that you understand the effects of home background on learning.

- Do you have to carry out an assignment or project involving small-scale research. You could design one as part of your course work and so kill two birds with one stone. If you are in a multicultural school look at your class list and that of another student. Make a form as in Figure 3.1 of the classes, setting out:

their NC levels for English;
their mother tongue;
the number of years they have been learning English;
whether they are on free school meals – a clear sign of poverty;
whether they are on the SEN register;
whether their parents are competent speakers of English;
whether the parents were educated in the UK.

The more classes and the greater range of classes with which you do this, the more reliable your results will be, but for the purpose of the course you will probably only have time to look at two or three classes.

You can then study the results and look for patterns from which you can draw conclusions. In analysing the results answer one or two of the following questions and suggest reasons for your conclusions.

1. Is a pupil's intellectual ability the main or only reason for success or failure within the system?
2. How does poverty (free school lunches) affect a child's progress?
3. Does it make a difference to a child who speaks English as an Additional Language (EAL) if their parents speak English or were educated in the UK?
4. Do the pupils who have been in the UK longer catch up or overtake the white British who were born here?
5. Does having lots of friends or no friends make a difference to the child's attitude to work and success as a learner?
6. What other factors play a part in influencing a pupil's learning?

When finishing your analysis, remember to add a paragraph stating that your findings are indicators of reasons for achievement or lack of it. Add that you must bear in mind that to be absolutely conclusive in your statements needs a survey of a few thousand pupils and is not within the scope of small-scale research.

Name of pupil	NC level of English	Mother tongue – English or other	Number of years learning English	SEN register (yes/no)	Parents fully competent in English (yes/no)	Parents educated in UK (0/1/2)	Has at least two friends in class (yes/no)

Figure 3.1

NB. You should only attempt the above if it also fulfils the requirement for an essay or other piece of academic work. You could not possibly afford the time for it otherwise.

Standard criteria
2.5 They know how to use ICT effectively, both to teach their subject and to support their wider professional role.

SUGGESTIONS FOR FULFILLING CRITERIA 2.5
Students do not usually need help with this one. I have not yet met anyone under 30 whose ICT skills were worse than mine.

- For history and geography, you can find an interesting website about a topic which the pupils are studying and make up a list of information for them to retrieve from it. This can often be done using cut and paste techniques.
- For science investigations, e.g. measuring the length of a shadow at different times of the day, let pupils construct a table on a spreadsheet on the computer to put in their findings and use them to construct a graph.
- For English, ask pupils to type the first draft of their essays or poems which you can then annotate with suggestions for improvement. I have found pupils very willing to edit their work to improve it without the painful task of rewriting it. When the task is complete let them look on the Internet, clip art or the school's files if appropriate to find illustrations. Secondary pupils can reference their illustrations.
- For poetry lessons, use www.google.com: Just type in 'poetry children' or 'poetry teenagers' and you will get a vast selection for pupils to read. I found www.gigglepoetry.com an effective site for getting Key Stage 2 reluctant learners started. They have interesting fun activities for making up poems and competitions.
- For maths there are games on the Internet, which you can download and print off on card and use. Try www.nrich.com for a selection of games and puzzles.
- There are also websites which prepare worksheets for lots of topics on the NC. I use www.primaryresources.co.uk. The BBC website www.bbc.co.uk/schools/revisewise is great for helping pupils to prepare for their exams.

- There are websites which give you NC lesson plans, e.g. Numeracy and Literacy Hour, Science and ICT plans. Many schools use info@skillsfactory.com.

To use ICT for your wider professional role:

- Type up your plans on the computer. Most schools have got a skeleton plan for you to type onto. This sometimes saves you time because if certain things are the same each week the next week's plan can be superimposed on it.
- It is better to type your schemes of work, reports and letters to parents. It looks more professional.
- Type labels for displays and add small pieces of clip art.
- If you prepare work at home you can email it from your home email address to your school email address. Some schools do not allow you to put plans on disk and bring them into the school in case you bring a virus into the school computer system.
- When you go on a school trip or school journey, take the school's digital camera and take lots of photos to download on the computer and use as a stimulus for discussion, to illustrate their work, use on a PowerPoint display in the class assembly or give to the pupils as souvenirs. Learn to use a projector. It's great for grabbing pupils' attention.
- Use PowerPoint to illustrate lessons or assemblies.
- Use spreadsheets with pupils' names and a list of skills or tasks to record what they have completed.

Standard criteria

2.6 They understand their responsibilities under the SEN Code of Practice and know how to seek advice from specialists in less common types of special educational needs.

SUGGESTIONS FOR FULFILLING CRITERIA 2.6

- This Code of Practice changes frequently so it will be important to read up the current document and the school's own SEN policy.
- Teachers have to write up targets each term/half-term for the pupils to achieve. You could ask the teacher to let you sit in

on the discussion to set them or let you be involved if you teach SEN pupils.

- Remember to put into your planning provision for children with special needs.
- Seek advice from the special educational needs coordinator (SENCO) on how to simplify the work for the SEN pupils.
- Ask the SENCO to explain what other provision the school makes for pupils with learning difficulties like dyslexia, dyspraxia and attention deficit hyperactivity disorder (ADHD).
- In your mark book, in the margin, write any detail of a pupil's health or educational needs: dyslexia, dyspraxia, ADHD, diabetes, asthma, epilepsy, serious food allergy.
- Find out which teacher is designated to deal with cases of suspected child abuse and ask him/her to explain the procedure.

Standard criteria

2.7 They know a range of strategies to promote good behaviour and establish a purposeful learning environment.

SUGGESTIONS FOR FULFILLING CRITERIA 2.7

- Early on in your placement, ask to read the school's behaviour policy because it is easier to control pupils if you are following the same set of rules as everyone else.
- Some teachers and students like to start with a class contract. They have discussion about what teacher and pupils expect from each other and they write it down on a poster and everyone agrees to stick to it. This is only suitable on teaching practice if you have the class regularly, and once you have done it you have to stick to your side of it otherwise it falls apart at once. Always ask advice from your mentor or the regular teacher before you start, because it is important to know how the teachers in the school normally do it.
- Make it clear from the start what you expect from the pupils by way of bringing the right books and equipment to class for each lesson.
- Try to start each lesson promptly. In a secondary school meet and greet the pupils at the door so that they cannot dawdle up the corridor.

- Make eye contact with all pupils as they walk past you. Speak positively to any pupils who look troubled or not their normal selves.
- Establish a clear homework policy and stick to it.
- Don't shout (if you can possibly avoid it). Noisy teachers have noisy classes.
- In a primary school, to get attention from a noisy class, say, 'Hands up those you are listening'. Say 'Well done' to the first six people who put their hands up. If it is an ultra-inattentive class, say, 'Well done you can go out at break-time' to the first six pupils.
- In a secondary school, you can establish a practice of saying, '3, 2, 1 and STOP'. Make it clear that you expect everyone's attention by the time you say '1', and anyone who is still moving or talking after you say 'STOP' will miss the first minute or two of the next break and carry it through.
- Never let one pupil spoil it for the whole class. For the disruptive pupil who is determined to wreck the class and ignores your warnings, you might say, 'You are clearly not in control of yourself and you are spoiling other pupils' opportunity to learn. Stand on the other side of the classroom door until you have calmed down and are capable of behaving like a mature Year 7 (or other) pupil. When you have done that you can return and we will say no more about it.'
- For classes who take a long time to tidy up at the end of a practical lesson establish a practice of letting the first group that is ready to go out for break-time a minute or two before the others.
- If necessary, reorganize seating so that pupils can be moved away from others who distract them from their work.
- Make sure all pupils are placed so that they can comfortably see the board.
- For the deliberately attention-seeking pupils, try to ignore the petty, negative behaviour (easier said than done, I know) and watch discreetly until they do the right thing. Then lavish praise on them.
- When a pupil is ignoring another who is trying to distract him/her praise the one who is behaving well. Reward

him/her with a star/sticker/house point, whatever is the norm in the school, and say how much you admire their cool attitude/grown-up behaviour/good sense in ignoring people who are silly.

- For the class that is reluctant to work, establish an incentive scheme, such as dividing them into four groups and letting them suggest a snazzy name for their own group. Then put up a chart with their names and give a reward at the end of the week or month for the group with the most points.
- For pupils who like to ignore the teacher, I have this system: ask politely, tell firmly, and then deliver a threat like a missed break-time and carry it out if necessary. It works most of the time after you have carried out the threat a time or two. If you keep pupils in for a whole break-time always let them out two minutes before the end to go to the loo,
- Keep the classroom tidy. Give pupils responsibilities for looking after different areas or types of equipment. Remember a disorderly environment sends out the message that the work is not important.
- Keep the notice-boards attractive, displaying the children's work neatly mounted with their name clearly displayed. This sends out the message that their work is valued and fosters a pride in their achievement (most of the time).

Standard criteria
2.8 They have passed the Qualified Teacher Status skills tests in numeracy, literacy and ICT.

SUGGESTIONS FOR FULFILLING CRITERIA 2.8
- Do the practise examples. Your tutor will advise you.
- Sort these out early on in the course. If you have any difficulties you will need extra time and practice so avoid putting yourself under unnecessary pressure by waiting.

3.1 Planning expectations and targets
Those awarded Qualified Teacher Status must demonstrate all of the following.

Standard criteria

3.1.1 They set challenging teaching and learning objectives which are relevant to all pupils in their classes. They base these on their knowledge of:
- the pupils
- evidence of their past and achievement
- the expected standards for pupils of the relevant age range
- the range and content of work relevant to pupils in that age range.

SUGGESTIONS FOR FULFILLING CRITERIA 3.1.1

You cannot possibly get this one right first time, so don't fall into the trap of thinking you are incompetent if it takes you a few lessons to get a clear picture of what the pupils can do.

- First ask the teacher for lots of information about what the pupils have already done and ask for suggestions for the next step.
- Look through a range of the pupils' exercise books to get an overall picture of the standard.
- Show the teacher your lesson plan and ask if there is anything you have left out or suggestions for improvement.
- Keep in mind that pupils pay most attention at the beginning and the end of the lesson, so make sure you have an interesting, attention-grabbing start and at the end sum up the main parts of the lesson.
- Make a note of any pupils, whom you think will need more practice and provide an extra activity for them. Often it's a good idea to start a lesson by recapping on the previous topic.

Standard criteria

3.1.2 They use these teaching and learning objectives to plan lessons, and sequences of lessons, showing how they will assess pupils' learning. They take account of and support pupils' varying needs so that girls and boys from all ethnic groups can make good progress.

SUGGESTIONS FOR FULFILLING CRITERIA 3.1.2

- Show your mentor a sample of schemes of work and lesson plans with objectives, differentiated work, evaluations, lesson observations.
- Start the lesson by writing the objective on the board and make sure the pupils know what it means. At the end of the lesson refer back to it and ask for an explanation. Praise warmly the pupils whom you believe have achieved the objective. (Mentally praise yourself for having achieved your objective with a substantial part of the class.)
- During each lesson, try to ask a question to every pupil. Be aware that in some classes boys grab more attention from the teacher than girls, and extrovert or confident pupils grab more attention than shy pupils. Try to avoid the imbalance of your time and attention.
- To pupils who are shy, give a few quiet words of encouragement as they walk out at the end of the lesson.

Standard criteria
3.1.3 They select and prepare resources, and plan for their safe and effective organization, taking account of pupils' interests and their language and cultural backgrounds.

SUGGESTIONS FOR FULFILLING CRITERIA 3.1.3
Many schools are well resourced so always examine the school's resources for your topic *before* you start making your own. Don't risk wasting precious time reinventing the wheel.

- For science examples, if it is an experiment which is new to you, do a dummy run first.
- If you are using anything potentially dangerous, e.g. chemicals in a secondary science lesson or boiling water in a primary science, hacksaws in DT lessons, look carefully at the school safety policy before you start. If you adhere to it you should be all right.
- Similarly, emphasize that when you ask for attention you must have it immediately as you might need to speak to pupils about a safety issue.
- Make sure there is a resource list on each lesson plan.

- Find out the school's procedure for using resources which are not standard in each classroom. Make sure where necessary that they are ordered in plenty of time and returned promptly.

Standard criteria

3.1.4 They take part in and contribute to teaching teams as appropriate to the school. Where applicable they plan for the deployment of additional adults who support pupils' learning.

SUGGESTIONS FOR FULFILLING CRITERIA 3.1.4

- It should be sufficient that you attend the planning meeting for your group in school. These can by tricky at first because sometimes experienced teachers (incorrectly) believe you cannot contribute a lot. The only answer is to persevere and the better the quality of your work the more they will welcome your suggestions.
- Make sure you write on all your plans the part played by each member of the support team and discuss it with them beforehand.
- When the lesson is over thank them for their help and ask if they were happy with what they were doing. Expressing your gratitude and showing them consideration often increases their support.
- Ask for advice and suggestions from the qualified support teachers if you can. Their feedback is often helpful.

Standard criteria

3.1.5 As relevant to the age range they are trained to teach, they are able to plan opportunities for pupils to learn in out-of-school contexts, such as school visits, museums, theatres, fieldwork and employment-based settings, with the help of other staff where appropriate.

SUGGESTIONS FOR FULFILLING 3.1.5

- Show your mentor notes and photographs of school trips where you have helped. Also the planning, risk assessment, letter to parents, timetable for the day, follow-up work.

- Offer to go on as many trips as you can. They are such an important part of pupils' education and they give you ideas for the future.
- If you can cope with the extra pressure on your time, offer to help with an after-school activity.

3.2 Monitoring and assessment
Those awarded Qualified Teacher Status must demonstrate all of the following.

Standard criteria
3.2.1 They make appropriate use of a range of monitoring and assessment strategies to evaluate pupils' progress towards planned learning objectives, and use this information to improve their own planning and teaching

SUGGESTIONS FOR FULFILLING 3.2.1
- On your record book have a system to record pupils' marks for the work or show whether each pupil has achieved the objective. (primary)
- On your lesson plans show that each lesson in the scheme begins by recapping on the previous one.
- On your lesson plans show how the information in your evaluation is reflected in the next lesson plan in the scheme.
- Show records of any assessments you have done at the end of units of work and how you have redone any work where the pupils needed extra practice.
- When handing back marked books show the class a couple of examples of pupils' work that show a good standard or improvement, and lavish praise on the pupil.
- For larger pieces of work which are ongoing ask pupils to set themselves a target for the next part of the project and look to see if they have tried to achieve it.

Standard criteria
3.2.2 They monitor and assess as they teach, giving immediate and constructive feedback to support pupils as they learn. They involve pupils in reflecting on, evaluating and improving their own performance.

SUGGESTIONS FOR FULFILLING 3.2.2

- When marking, write constructive comments after each piece of work, where appropriate setting a pertinent target for the pupil to try to achieve in their next piece of work.
- Ask pupils to set a target for themselves at the beginning of each half-term and check it at the end of the half-term if you are there that long.
- At the end of each term/half-term ask them to write a self assessment of how well they think they have progressed. Give them headings such as 'What I have done well' 'What I need to improve' 'What I enjoyed' 'What I didn't enjoy'.
- Give positive reinforcement throughout lessons where appropriate and constructive suggestions for improvement. If you have done this well, an observer should have noted it in their written feedback.

Standard criteria

3.2.3 They are able to assess pupils' progress accurately using, as relevant, the Early Learning Goals, NC level descriptions, criteria from national qualifications, the requirements of Awarding Bodies, NC and Foundation Stage assessment frameworks or objectives from the National Strategies. They may have guidance from an experienced teacher where appropriate.

SUGGESTIONS FOR FULFILLING CRITERIA 3.2.3

- Keep a record of all the moderation meetings you have attended.
- Show samples of pupils' work you have assessed for its NC level. Annotate the work to show which level descriptors the pupils have achieved.
- Show your mark book with levels pupils have achieved with samples of work to illustrate each level.

Standard criteria

3.2.4 They identify and support more able pupils, those who are working below age-related expectations, those who are failing to achieve their potential in learning, and those who experience behavioural, emotional and social difficulties.

They may have guidance from an experienced teacher where appropriate.

SUGGESTIONS FOR FULFILLING 3.2.4
- Read the school's SEN policy with regard to supporting the more able, and the inclusion of refugees and asylum seekers. (They are frequently underachievers.)
- Show your mentor examples of extension work you have prepared for the more able.
- Show on your lesson plan where you have made provision for the SEN pupils.
- Show your mentor as evidence:
  - IEPs you have produced and taught
  - records of meetings you have had with the SENCO, EAL co-ordinator and other professionals who are involved with the pupils
  - records of disciplinary action and incident forms.
- In your weekly meeting with your mentor ask for advice on how to cater for specific pupils.

Standard criteria
3.2.5 With the help of an experienced teacher, they can identify the levels of attainment of pupils learning English as an additional language. They begin to analyse the language demands and learning activities in order to provide cognitive challenge as well as language support.

SUGGESTIONS FOR FULFILLING 3.2.5
- Read the school's EAL policy.
- Read the criteria for each level of achievement in English. The EAL coordinator can give you a copy.
- Ask your mentor to clarify any points that are not clear.
- Show an example of pupils' work at each level to demonstrate your understanding of the level descriptions.
- Show your mentor as evidence records of meetings you have had with the EAL coordinator or any other professional involved with EAL pupils.
- Liaise with the EAL staff when planning lessons for classes which include EAL pupils.

- In your mark book include a column for the pupils' levels of English.
- Provide as evidence lesson plans showing provision for EAL pupils.
- Look at the suggestions in 3.3.5 below for suggestions to facilitate EAL pupils' learning.

Standard criteria

3.2.6 They record pupils' progress and achievements systematically to provide evidence of the range of their work, progress and attainment over time. They use this to help pupils review their own progress and to inform planning.

SUGGESTIONS FOR FULFILLING 3.2.6

- Provide as evidence your mark book, series of lesson plans and lesson observations.
- Show your mentor the pupils' books, marked with advice given to show if pupils have acted on advice in earlier pieces of work.

Standard criteria

3.2.7 They are able to use records as a basis for reporting on pupils' attainment and progress orally and in writing, concisely, informatively and accurately for parents, carers, other professionals and pupils.

SUGGESTIONS FOR FULFILLING 3.2.7

- The school should have a system to record pupils' progress. As long as you follow their system this should satisfy your college supervisor.
- Show your mentor as evidence:
  - copies of school reports you have written for parents
  - copies of reports and input made into referrals for Heads of Year, Educational Psychologist, Educational Welfare Officer
  - notes from any meetings you have had on parents' evening or other meetings with parents.
- If you attend a parents' evening, you might use your record of pupils' marks to give weight to your comments where appropriate.

3.3 Teaching and class management

Those awarded Qualified Teacher Status must demonstrate all of the following.

Standard criteria

3.3.1 They have high expectations of pupils and build successful relationships, centred on teaching and learning. They establish a purposeful learning environment where diversity is valued and where pupils feel secure and confident.

SUGGESTIONS FOR FULFILLING 3.3.1

- Use your lecturer's observation notes as evidence of good relationships.
- On your record book show that homework is given in on time or late. Show pupils individually where you keep a record of it and remind them that it will be noted if their work is consistently late.
- Show your mentor as evidence examples of good quality pupils' work and examples of resources you have made.
- Make a display of high quality pupils' work. Make sure the display represents the diversity of pupils.

Standard criteria

3.3.2 They can teach the required or expected knowledge, understanding and skills relevant to the curriculum for pupils in the age range for which they are trained. In relation to specific phases:
  (a) Foundation Stage – teach all six areas of learning outlined in the QCA/DfES Curriculum Guidance for Foundation Stage, and for Reception children, the objectives of the National Literacy and Numeracy Strategy frameworks competently and independently.

SUGGESTIONS FOR FULFILLING 3.3.2(A)

- Provide as evidence lesson plans and evaluations for each of the curriculum areas, observation notes for lessons, lesson plans for regular Numeracy and Literacy Hours.
- Ask your mentor for more ideas to develop your work. Asking is evidence of your determination to keep on developing your skills.

Standard criteria

3.3.2(b) Those qualifying to teach pupils in Key Stage 1 and/or 2 teach the core subjects (English, including the National Literacy Strategy, mathematics through the National Numeracy Strategy, and science) competently and independently.

They also teach, for either Key Stage 1 or Key Stage 2, a range of work across the following subjects: history or geography; physical education; ICT; art and design or design and technology and performing arts independently, with advice from an experienced colleague where appropriate.

SUGGESTIONS FOR FULFILLING 3.3.2(B)

- Provide your lesson plans for the above lessons.
- Make sure that on each plan you put in the correct NC reference and any observation notes and evaluations.

Standard criteria

3.3.2(c) Those qualifying to teach Key Stage 3 pupils teach their specialist subject(s) competently and independently using the NC Programmes of Study for Key Stage 3 and the relevant national frameworks and schemes of work. Those qualifying to teach the core subjects or ICT at Key Stage 3 use the relevant frameworks, methods and expectations set out in the National Strategy for Key Stage 3. All those qualifying to teach a subject at Key Stage 3 must be able to use the cross-curricular elements, such as literacy and numeracy, set out in the National Strategy for Key Stage 3, in their teaching, as appropriate to their specialist subject.

SUGGESTIONS FOR FULFILLING 3.3.2(C)

- Produce as evidence lesson plans with NC references and your own schemes of work with worksheets.
- In your plans show where you have conferred with other departments to provide cross-curricular lessons, e.g. art/history, art/RE, English/history.

Standard criteria

3.3.2(d) Those qualifying to teach Key Stage 4 and post-16 pupils teach their specialist subject(s) competently and independently using, as relevant to the subject and age range, the NC Programmes of Study and related schemes of work, or programmes specified for national qualifications. They also provide opportunities for pupils to develop the key skills specified by QCA.

SUGGESTIONS FOR FULFILLING 3.3.2(D)

- Show on your lesson plans where they relate directly to the exam specification.
- Show your lesson plans with NC references and your own schemes of work with worksheets.

Standard criteria

3.3.3 They teach clearly structured lessons or sequences of work which interest and motivate pupils and which;
  - make learning objectives clear to pupils
  - employ interactive teaching methods and collaborative group work
  - promote active and independent learning that enables pupils to think for themselves, and to plan and manage their own learning.

SUGGESTIONS FOR FULFILLING 3.3.3

- Write your learning objective on the board at the start of each lesson and make sure pupils know what it means.
- At the end of each lesson refer back to the objective and ask questions to test if the objective has been achieved.
- Organize lessons which involve mixed ability groups in problem-solving and fact-finding.
- Give homework tasks which involve pupils consulting books, and the Internet, to find information for themselves.
- Pupils, even secondary, love games. Use them to reinforce points to be learnt.

Standard criteria

3.3.4 They differentiate their teaching to meet the needs of pupils, including the more able and those with special educational needs. They may have guidance from an experienced teacher where appropriate.

SUGGESTIONS FOR FULFILLING 3.3.4

- Show lesson plans, showing clearly the role of the CA, SEN or EAL support teacher.
- Provide examples of differentiated work – extension work for the more able and simplified for the less able.
- Provide any information sheets which have been simplified for the pupils.

Standard criteria

3.3.5 They are able to support those who are learning English as an additional language, with the help of an experienced teacher where appropriate.

SUGGESTIONS FOR FULFILLING 3.3.5

- Consult the EAL coordinator before you start. They are usually full of sound practical suggestions. They will probably have lots of resources which you can use. (As always, avoid reinventing the wheel.)
- Start each lesson by explaining the key vocabulary.
- Give practical demonstrations where possible. They are so much more meaningful to the EAL pupils.
- As far as possible allow pupils in the early stages of English to sit beside a pupil who can translate for them.
- For teaching of reading (primary or secondary) try to find dual text books. They are a godsend to the EAL pupil.
- If there is a bilingual teacher or assistant in the school ask him/her to write the text of your worksheet in the child's own language. Of course you have to check that the child can read his/her own language first.
- When they start to talk don't start correcting every single mistake in their speech. It puts them right off. They will pick up the right grammar and vocabulary the longer they are in the UK.
- Likewise, when they start to write, don't correct every single error. The bits you do correct, do it in the same colour as the pupil has used. 'Encouragement' is the keyword, not strict accuracy in the first instance.

Standard criteria

3.3.6 They take account of the varying interests, experiences and achievements of boys and girls, and pupils from different cultural and ethnic groups, to help pupils make good progress.

SUGGESTIONS FOR FULFILLING 3.3.6
- In your register, make notes of pupils' known interests, ethnic groups and religion.
- Where appropriate introduce the above into lessons.

Standard criteria

3.3.7 They organize and manage teaching and learning time effectively.

SUGGESTIONS FOR FULFILLING 3.3.7
- Show a timetable for the lesson on each lesson plan.

Standard criteria

3.3.8 They organize and manage the physical teaching space, tools, materials, texts and other resources safely and effectively with the help of support staff where appropriate.

SUGGESTIONS FOR FULFILLING 3.3.8
- Show the resource list on the teaching plan.
- Where resources have to be ordered, make sure you do so in plenty of time and return them quickly after use.
- Make sure you observe any safety rules, e.g. relating to chemicals or technology tools.
- At the end of practical lessons using a lot of equipment, build a clearing up time into the lesson plan.

Standard criteria

3.3.9 They set high expectations for pupils' behaviour and establish a clear framework for classroom discipline.

SUGGESTIONS FOR FULFILLING 3.3.9
- In your first lesson with each class, set out your parameters and give reasons. Some students (and teachers) spend the first 15 minutes negotiating a contract.

- Impress on pupils when appropriate that disruption to a lesson is unfair and harmful to the other pupils.
- Use the school policy for behaviour management.
- When in difficulty always consult the regular teacher for advice. This is not a sign of weakness. It is common sense.

Standard criteria
3.3.10 They use ICT effectively in their teaching.

SUGGESTIONS FOR FULFILLING 3.3.10

- Show on your lesson plans where you have asked the pupils to research topics on the Intenet.
- Give examples of your own resource and information sheets taken from the Internet.
- You may be lucky and have access to a smart board for a few lessons.
- Lessons using PowerPoint. They always impress.
- Prepare your lesson plans and worksheets on the computer.

Standard criteria
3.3.11 They can take responsibility for teaching a class or classes over a sustained and substantial period of time. They are able to teach across the age and ability range for which they are trained.

SUGGESTIONS FOR FULFILLING 3.3.11

- Your timetable and file of lesson plans alone should fulfil this one adequately as long as you have recorded the differentiated work to show you can cope with the range of ability.

Standard criteria
3.3.12 They can provide homework and other out-of-class work which consolidates and extends work carried out in the class and encourages pupils to learn independently.

SUGGESTIONS FOR FULFILLING 3.3.12

- Record the homework set on your lesson plans.
- Include activities of the 'Find out as much as you can about . . .' type.

- Make it necessary for pupils to go to the library, surf the net.

Standard criteria

3.3.13 They work collaboratively with specialist teachers and other colleagues and, with the help of an experienced teacher as appropriate, manage the work of teaching assistants or other adults to enhance pupils' learning.

SUGGESTIONS FOR FULFILLING 3.3.13

- Records of meetings with specialists. Include the advice they have offered and show in your lesson plans how you have used it.
- On the plan show the CA's role and give him/her a copy of the lesson plan.

Standard criteria

3.3.14 They recognize and respond effectively to equal opportunities issues as they arise in the classroom, including by challenging stereotyped views, and by challenging bullying or harassment, following relevant policies and procedures.

SUGGESTIONS FOR FULFILLING 3.3.14

- Read the school's anti-bullying policy, and apply it when the situation arises. Make a written record of any such occurrences.
- Challenge any stereotyping in class.
- In class make sure you do not allow the more vibrant members of the class to take up most of your time and attention.
- Make a conscious effort to address a similar number of questions to each pupil.
- Where appropriate use role models of women and non-Europeans. Avoid the 'dead white European male' syndrome.

And when you have waded your way through this little lot reward yourself with a terrific night out!

4 The Side Issues

Stress Management

What is stress?

According to my dictionary, stress is mental and physical distress or anxiety caused by difficult circumstances. It is not something imagined by students and others. It is real and some students suffer it so badly that students at Cambridge University have named the Sunday after the exams finish as 'Suicide Sunday'.

Today's students probably suffer from it more than students in previous generations, because of the added pressures of finding cash to pay their fees and keep, and the thought of their loans hanging over them like a sword of Damocles long after they qualify. On the other hand there are more systems in place now so that students get help before they reach crisis point.

What causes stress to students?

These are a few of the difficult circumstances which cause suffering to students:

- Being unable to finish assignments or dissertations on time.
- Fearing you cannot understand the work or present essays of high enough quality.
- Dreading not being able to manage the pupils the next day on your school placement.
- Coping with the workload on teaching practice. As soon as you shift one pile of marking, another appears.
- Lack of support in schools.
- Fearing the reaction of your family if you fail.
- Living in unpleasant accommodation.
- Money problems.

- Having family problems – unruly children, illness in the family, bereavement.
- Discovering that there is a shortage of jobs for your area of study (fortunately at present this is not usually a problem for student teachers).

Stress is usually caused by a mixture of some of the above.

How do you recognize the signs?

A small amount of stress in our lives keeps us all moving, working and achieving, but there is a limit to how much of it we can tolerate and when we have substantially more that we can cope with, it makes us ill.

Unlike a dose of a normal disease, stress creeps up on you so slowly that you don't know it is happening until it is too late. It is important to recognize the signs in time and try to avoid the resulting unhappiness. It is also worth being aware of the frame of mind of people around you so that if one of your friends or colleagues is suffering it, you may be able to step in and help them.

Stress takes different forms but these are common symptoms:

- frequent headaches;
- extreme tiredness;
- a feeling of powerlessness;
- fear that your life is out of control;
- experiencing panic attacks at times;
- wanting to cry or actually sitting down and doing it at inappropriate times;
- feeling depressed – morbidly unhappy with a mood of inadequacy;
- feeling that life is not worth living.

How do you avoid stress?

BEING ORGANIZED IS CRUCIAL

A lot of stress is caused by poor time management and weak organizational skills.

When you are given a new essay or assignment it is important to consult the calendar before the textbooks. Look up the date for handing it in and plan ahead. Aim to finish with at least a week to spare because these things often take longer than you expect.

You should also build into your timetable a few days to reread, check and amend it. Also remember that if lots of students are reliant on textbooks in the library, it is unwise to leave it until the last week because the books will be in demand.

If you have written an essay or completed an assignment but are not feeling confident about it, some lecturers are willing to read students' work if they have it in time and tell them where they have gone wrong, or could make a few improvements or even just give the reassurance that the essay is fine. Of course it is important to give the lecturer the work well in advance of the deadline date, and it is well worth it for the peace of mind.

During teaching practice self-organization becomes doubly important because if you don't sort out your lessons and resources you will lose control and credibility and become stressed and grease the slippery slope to failure. Before you leave each day, it is a sensible precaution to make sure you are prepared for the following day's lessons. Never live hand-to-mouth because you will always find things which you cannot do at the last minute and you will wish you had sorted them out sooner.

ROUTINE

Plan out your week. Having times designated for socializing and times for working is much better than just taking each day as it comes or waiting until you are in the mood for working. On teaching practice, build a marking and planning space into the daily routine.

When facing up to the fact that you might not have much spare time for yourself during the week, make sure you set aside time at the weekends and holidays. It is important to learn to shut school or college out of your mind for a period every weekend to enable you to return to the job refreshed.

HALF-TERM

If you have one, set aside a bit of time to relax and enjoy yourself and come back refreshed. Try not to lose sight of the big picture. You are training to be a teacher so that you can live; not the other way round.

ONLY DO WHAT IS NECESSARY

It's the quality of work and the relevance of the work that counts. Not the number of hours you spend on it. This doesn't mean you can cut corners or do the least you can get away with. Work out what is necessary to plan and deliver the lessons or write the essays properly and leave it at that. Do the necessary stuff first and don't allow yourself the luxury of delving into anything else just because it looks interesting. Just as in office work or running a home, you have to prioritize.

DON'T LET ANY OF YOUR WORK GO TO WASTE

Remember the filing cabinet. Whatever you have taught, you are bound to teach it again one day. All copies of lesson plans, medium- and long-term plans and the accompanying worksheets should be in a paper wallet, clearly marked with the subject or Key Stage. Knowing where everything is is vital because there is no point in keeping it if you have to spend ages looking for it.

Nor should you let what you have learnt go to waste. Try to feed what you have learnt back into your planning and practice in the classroom. It gives you a tremendous feeling of satisfaction to see that you have achieved that goal of putting theory into practice and the feel-good factor helps to counteract stress.

NEVER WORK WHEN YOU ARE TIRED

It is impossible to achieve anything worthwhile when you have a hammer banging away inside your head. All you will achieve is a headache and a lot of poor quality 'work'. It is far better to go to bed and sleep, possibly getting up earlier the next morning and doing the work with a clear head.

Try to find what is your optimal working period in the day. Some people function better in the early morning after a night's sleep when their head is clear. I know one student who wrote her dissertation by regularly getting up early when the house was quiet, and working between 5 and 7 o'clock each morning. Some people get a 'second wind' late at night and after a strong cup of coffee can have two productive hours. It is important to know what is your best period in the day and capitalize by trying to do your most difficult work then.

What do you do when you have stress?

DON'T STRUGGLE ALONG ON YOUR OWN

Talk to your partner, if you have one, and impress on him/her that you are just plain unable to cope with the current lifestyle and need help and support to get back to normal. If you are single, parents or friends may be your life-line.

THE STUDENT COUNSELLING SERVICE

Most universities have a student counselling service. They are accustomed to supporting students through the difficulties so go along to see them. They may be able to give you advice on how to get yourself back on track.

GET MEDICAL HELP

If you start feeling a few of the symptoms mentioned above, the first step is to recognize that you are stressed and acknowledge that your health is more important than your studies, exams, lesson plans, keeping the house tidy and getting your dissertation in on time. Insisting on struggling on will make you much worse and put off your restoration to good health. If you are feeling weepy, snapping at people, unable to sleep and wanting to smoke or drink too much, go first to your supervisor/tutor/mentor and explain your work-related problems.

Then go straight to the doctor and tell him/her your symptoms and describe your hectic life, and with a bit of luck s/he will write you off ill for a week or two or three.

TREAT THE CAUSE BEFORE THE SYMPTOMS

You must also work out what is the cause of your stress and treat the cause, not the symptoms. Look at the list of causes above and ask yourself which apply to you. There will probably be more than one or there may be others not mentioned. Try to pinpoint exactly what causes your stress and then you can start trying to work out how to get rid of it.

COLLEGE WORK

If you cannot get through your college work in time, don't be afraid to ask your tutor for an extension, perhaps into the holidays to give you more time. This is not a sign of weakness. Many students do it every year and lecturers much prefer you to give the work in later than crack up and not finish the course.

Sometimes students find the college work difficult to understand and are not confident to speak out in lectures and seminars to ask for explanations. I know a few who managed to overcome this with private tuition. It was costly but in the long run it was money well spent.

Sometimes students come out of exams, or even re-sits, fearing or knowing they have failed. The fear of telling their family who are proud of them becomes so great in their mind that they become stressed. There have been a few dreadfully distressing, extreme cases where students have committed suicide, probably too wrapped up in their anxiety to realize that their sad death would cause infinitely more grief than their failure at university.

Needless to say it is important for every student to recognize their importance in their parents' lives and to face up to telling them the facts. If you cannot do it face to face, a phone call, a letter or email is all right. Students must remember that their parents are not young and vulnerable. They are middle-aged and have had enough life experience to toughen them up to take life's little knocks. Most students find that their parents, though disappointed, are quite sympathetic and prepared to support them through the phase while they have time out, repeat the year or find a job.

SCHOOL WORK

Some students (and teachers) are afraid to say that they cannot cope in case they look weak. This is unwise, because teachers always know if someone is not coping and they admire them less for pretending otherwise.

If you are finding it hard to cope in the school where you have your placement, look carefully at your timetable. Are you being asked to do more than the stipulated percentage of the timetable? Also look at your individual classes. Have they given you a class (or two) which is difficult to manage, one which everyone hates? There is one in most schools and it is unfair to land it on a student unless they give you a lot of support. In either case, you must point this out to the head or head of department, whichever has the power to reduce your workload. Also talk to your mentor and your college supervisor if you are not getting enough support.

Similarly, it may be that you have voluntarily taken on too much. Students and newly qualified teachers often do not realize how much the job involves until they are up to their ears in it. If you have taken on anything voluntarily and find you cannot cope, you will just have to say so and cut out the extra work.

If you have attended the doctor and are taking medication, make sure you tell them so. It is now an offence to cause stress to people at work and some employees have successfully sued their employer for it. Although you are not an employee, no one would want to be accused of causing anxiety to a student.

ACCOMMODATION PROBLEMS

Living somewhere which is unpleasant or sharing with people with whom you cannot get on can add stress to a student's life. I have known students to sort out the problem by packing their bags and returning to the comfort of the family home. Of course you can only do that if you live within convenient travelling distance of your college.

If this is not the case then you must make an appointment to see whoever is in charge of student accommodation, tell him/her your problem and ask for help to find somewhere to live. Again, say that it is causing you stress and you have been to the doctor and are taking medication. To strengthen your case, make a list of dates and times to show frequency of the problems you are experiencing. It makes sure you are taken seriously.

FAMILY PROBLEMS

Family problems can come in all shapes and sizes and at any time of your life. You can always get compassionate leave if there is a bereavement in the family. A severe illness in the family can cause so much stress that students are unable to study. In cases like this, universities normally take a compassionate view and allow the student to take even a whole year off, to return home and resume their studies the following year.

Small children sometimes give their parents grief if they do not get enough attention when parents are too preoccupied with their job or studies. You have got to impress on your partner that you need extra support and if you are a single parent this is where you must call on the support of the extended family. Don't try to be an island. That's what families are for – to look after each other. If there are no family around, you may have to turn to friends to help you with childcare. Or if your doctor prescribes time off you will be able to give your children a bit more care yourself for a while.

At this point some young parents on teacher training begin to worry that although they like teaching they may not be able to cope with it while childrearing. One option is to work part-time after the induction year and then build up to working full-time as the children become more independent after a few years.

Now treat the symptoms

Even if you have taken some steps to remove the cause of your anxiety, you might still have that uncomfortable feeling of being tense and wound up. Many people have their own way of regaining that laid-back feeling.

Some find relief in attending a yoga class and practising the art of relaxation and others find sitting quietly in a dark room listening to gentle classical music to be a relaxant. Exercise brings back the feel-good factor. Many people enjoy an hour or two working out in the gym and others love to play a vigorous game of squash or badminton. Swimming is a great way to remove all of the tension from your body because you use most or all of your muscles; some find the same effect going for a jog.

For those who are not sporty but still want some exercise in a pleasant, non-competitive atmosphere an evening class for some sort of lively dancing might help – Scottish, Irish or English country dancing all get the blood flowing more quickly.

Even a brisk walk at the end of a day's work helps you to feel better. Getting off the bus or train a stop early and walking can get rid of stress before you get home.

Don't forget the big picture

Always keep it at the front of your mind that your student days are short. Even three or four years is a very minor portion of your life. Remember that many students have suffered and eventually coped with the anxieties you may be feeling. This is a temporary phase and you will probably be so busy that each week will fly past you and when you finally walk onto the platform to receive your degree you will be wondering where the time has gone.

Balancing the Course and Family Life

Teacher training is very demanding. Even if you are young and single and have no family commitments, it takes some perseverance to get through the course. If you have a partner and children the task of coping with family life and your course becomes very complex. Your success as a parent and student is co-measurate with your ability to balance the two tasks.

Having a baby while at college

Some student teachers do become pregnant while still at college. This is less difficult if you are further into the course, because by this time you have become accustomed to the student way of working.

Pregnancy is something female students have to consider very seriously because it creates so many logistical difficulties. Even if you are a male student you need to plan your family carefully, because a birth during the exam period could mean the difference between passing and failing, given the chances of sleep loss. Think twice about it, because it is far from easy.

Few colleges have crèches and you may not be able to afford a childminder, so some neo-mothers may have to take their babies into college with them and hope they stay silent or sleep through lectures.

The main problem – loss of sleep – can make studying and absorbing anything during lectures really difficult. One of my colleagues who was a successful student, teacher and mum, coped by turning up for college each day to get her attendance mark, sitting through the lectures half asleep with her baby strapped to her, and her dictaphone on so that she could listen to the lecture later, at home, when the baby was in bed. If you can get away with doing this, it would be wise to sit near the door to make a quick getaway if the baby howls.

What are the difficulties and how do you cope?

Quality time with the family

You will have much less time to spend with your family.

Talk to your partner before you start. Make sure s/he understands that you will have a heavy workload, will not be able to put the same amount of time and energy into your marriage/relationship until the course is over and that you will need support to get through it. Unless you have the wholehearted support of your partner you are unlikely to stick it out to the end.

Travelling can take up a lot of time. It is important to take a course as close to home as you can manage. You still need to study the course in detail to make sure it is what you want and this can lead to your balancing the course you might prefer against the one which will save you ten hours of travelling time each week.

Children accept change better if the reasons for it are clear. Explain that you are going back to school and like them you will have homework and will not have quite so much time to spend enjoying their company. Tell them how long it will go on, if they are old enough to understand, because they like to know what's happening, and explain the advantage that when it finishes you will have a good job and much more money to spend on their birthday and Christmas presents, holidays and their maintenance at university. Children and teenagers are very open to promises of rewards and downright bribery.

With everyone in the family being pulled in every direction, it is hard to find time to do things together, but it is worth trying, where possible, to have meals together. It is not until teenagers leave home and find themselves eating alone, filling themselves with junk food or the institutionalized meals of the refectory that they appreciate the atmosphere of the cooked family meal at home.

Routine is also important. Children like to know where they stand: who is picking them up from school, looking after them, helping them with their homework. If you have someone different picking up your child from school don't forget to tell the teacher as well as your child because some schools have a policy not to release the child otherwise. Having a similar routine each week reduces frustration for both you and your children.

Try to find some time in the weekend when the family can spend time together doing something completely different. It helps you get things into perspective and, remember, there is more to life than work and studying.

Childcare

This is the most common problem in families where both parents go out to work or study. Of course having a full-time nanny is ideal but most people, especially students, cannot afford one. Sometimes two families get together and share a nanny to make it more affordable. Others solve the problem by having an au pair, but if you haven't got a spare bedroom that's not possible.

Some young parents are in the happy position of having nearby grandparents to mind the baby or take the children to school or nursery and pick them up. Grandparents are wonderful. They do not complain if you change arrangements, and do not ask for extra payment if you are late. In fact some do not ask for payment at all, and you can go to college secure in the knowledge that your child is being treated with loving care. However it is unlikely that they will want the job of minding your children full-time and so you will need to negotiate carefully with them as they have lives and interests too. One day per week seems fairly reasonable. Their goodwill will last longer if you do not take advantage of them.

FINDING A CHILDMINDER

If your children are too young to go to nursery then you will have to find a childminder. Local councils keep a list but of course you will prefer personal recommendation.

When you first visit it is best to take your baby with you to see how they respond to each other. I would also go during a working day so that you could see what other children she minds and decide whether you are happy with your child being with her. Some parents will only leave their child with a minder who takes no others but I always liked there to be other children so that mine could become accustomed to the company.

You will probably use your own intuition to judge if it is a happy, caring home but you must also note if the home looks clean and safe and if there is cigarette smoke in the atmosphere. Ask questions about their daily routine; some childminders take their children to the local mum and baby group and some to the local gym or swimming pool where they have a mother and toddler session.

It is best to check that she is registered with the local council and of course ask to see her latest inspection report. Childminders have to suffer the eagle eyes of Ofsted as well. Ask her for the names and telephone numbers of past parents so that you can contact them to take up references.

If you advertise you might be lucky and find a young parent who is willing to bring her child to your home and look after them both together. This will be more expensive but a lot more convenient and your child will have the comfort of having his/her own toys around all day and won't have to suffer the discomfort of being taken out in the cold in winter. If you are in this fortunate position don't forget to check that the minder is registered with the local council.

Separation during teaching practice

You could be very unfortunate and have one of your teaching practice placements away from home so you would only see the family at the weekend when you are tired and have work to do.

As soon as you get settled into the course, find out who is in charge of organizing the teaching practice placements and approach them to explain that you have children and would be grateful to be placed in a school within easy travelling distance of home. Lecturers have told me they try to be amenable about that.

The workload

As stated earlier the course is intensive and the workload amounts to a full-time job. Some mature students find courses where the training is part-time and so it is easier to combine it with running the home and bringing up the children, but of course it will last longer if done like this.

This is where the family comes in. You will already have warned your partner that you will have less time and need his/her support. Cut the housework to the bare minimum – dusting and hoovering once a week, maximum.

Sit down with your partner and write down the tasks which are an absolute necessity – taking younger children to school and picking them up, clothes laundered, meals prepared. Decide who does each one and start a routine because jobs are then less likely to be left undone if they are delegated.

If you can afford it get a domestic cleaning person. Two hours once or twice a week can get the dusting, hoovering and ironing done and take the strain off you both. They are not expensive and if you ask around you can usually find one as most full-time working mothers have one these days. If you cannot find one, an advertisement in a shop 'nosy board' or local library usually brings several replies.

Ask your older children to help by taking on little jobs around the house, acccording to their age and ability. As long as they are not up to their ears in studying for GCSEs or worse, they are often quite amenable. Taking responsibility and being shown proper appreciation for it gives them self-esteem and I found that offering extra pocket money for chores around the home always worked.

Making technology work for you

Today's technology is a godsend to the household where both parents are working. Most areas in the UK have a delivery service from a nearby supermarket. Shopping online can save you hours of tedious supermarket shelf wandering. Most of them show the bargains on the screen so you don't lose out and the delivery charge is not a waste of money because you will save litres of petrol by eliminating the journey. It's also a great time-saver to buy Christmas, birthday and wedding presents.

Microwaves are another boon. Your teenage children will not always be able to make it on time for every meal. In fact teenagers, on principle, have to be different to demonstrate their growing maturity. They will appreciate being able to reheat their evening meal in two minutes and you will not suffer the irritation of watching a nutritious meal being spoilt by being left for an hour or two.

A freezer saves you time. You can cook in bulk at the weekend and use the microwave to reheat it during the week. It doesn't spoil the taste if done properly. In fact some meals, like curries, improve in taste. Buying in bulk and storing in the freezer also saves time on shopping, and saves money.

If you can afford a dishwasher it will also save time, especially if loading it and unloading it could be the children's job.

Exam time

There can be no doubt that performance in exams, in fact anything, is enhanced by an alert state of mind. You should make sure your children understand that you must be in bed early, even if it means going to bed before your older children. This has the added advantage that it sets them an example because they take you more seriously if you have been seen to practise what you have preached to them.

Enlist your children's sympathy. If they have done a few exams themselves you can appeal to their good nature, with comments like 'You know what it's like, dear, I just have to concentrate on them to make sure I pass'. If they are too young to understand, try 'It's only for a short time until my exams are over'. Then promise a fun day out when the exams are finished.

If tiredness prevents you from studying, get your partner to keep the children quiet or take them out on a Saturday or Sunday afternoon while you go to bed. There is nothing like a sleep in the afternoon to set you up for a productive evening.

A few tips to get through it:

- Ask the cleaning lady to do a few extra hours during the exam period.
- If there is a school holiday in the weeks before the exams ask around the extended family if some kind aunt, uncle or grandparents would have your children for a few days 'holiday'.
- It's better to study in the library if there are too many distractions at home.
- Make it clear to your family you can't be asked to do anything extra for them until the exams are over.
- Never skimp on food. Proper, nutritious meals keep your energy levels up and stop you becoming ill when you are under pressure. Try to get your partner or older children to do the cooking. Failing that, only have meals with short preparation time or buy some fish and chips or other takeaway if you can afford it.
- Keep your vitamin C levels and Omega oil levels up to avoid colds.
- Stress can cause headaches. Keep the painkillers handy, and drink plenty of water because stress dehydrates.
- If your children are stroppy, let your partner handle it.

PREPARING FOR THE EXAMS

- Sit down with your friends at college and look at some old exam papers. Some people are clever at spotting topics which come up regularly.

- Share the load. Sometimes students get together and study different parts of the syllabus and share their notes. Of course you can only do this with people you can trust.
- Try out an old exam paper under exam conditions. Your tutor might be willing to read your answers and offer some advice.

Money problems

If you have given up a job to do the course, this will mean a cut in your weekly budget. It is best to sit down with your partner and work out how much less money you will have and how you will downsize your budget to cope with the shortfall. Sometimes this means cutting out holidays, the trips to the cinema, theatre and restaurants.

Try not to make the mistake of skimping on food. It's a very false economy because it reduces your ability to cope and you are more likely to become ill.

At the weekend it is tempting to think you cannot go anywhere or do anything because you are short of cash. There are lots of things you can do that do not need money. A trip to the local park to play on the swings and roundabouts or a game of football or cricket with their dad is just as much fun to children as a trip to the cinema and costs nothing.

Just because you cannot afford aeroplane fares and hotels abroad, does not mean you cannot afford holidays. There are plenty of places in Britain with campsites. Children love camping because it seems like an adventure to them. You don't have to spoil it for yourself by doing lots of shopping and cooking. There are often cafés close by or you can resort to fish and chips or take-aways.

Don't forget there is some financial help for students. Look at the section on funding in Chapter 1 or visit the website www.tta.gov.uk/fundingfortrainees for up-to-date information.

Keeping your sanity

Keep reminding yourself that the situation is temporary. Most people in this situation say the advantages far outweigh the drawbacks. When you are qualified, you will still have to work hard but you will have more money and you will not have to cope with the strain of exams and being permanently judged, and you will feel more secure.

There will probably be other mature students on the course who have children. Make friends with them and you can encourage and support each other. You might be able to team up with them during the school holidays. A trip to the local swimming pool or pantomime is more fun when you share it with another family.

Take time out at the end of each term to enjoy the company of other students. There's usually a party or a meal out at the end of each term or the occasional night in the pub during the term. Try not to rush home quickly to the family every night because a change can be as beneficial as a rest and you deserve it now and again.

When it's over
Now is the time to reward yourself and your family. Have a family treat like a special night out, a visit to a theme park or a weekend away. Make it clear to your children that you appreciate their support during the course and this is to reward them for helping you through it.

Once the prospect of a larger income is secure, you can sit down with your partner and enjoy the luxury of being able to plan how to improve the quality of life for your family.

5 Getting Ready for the Real World

Finding your First Job

An inescapable hurdle – not to be underestimated

This is quite an exciting task. After the long years of study, students feel they are finally about to reach their goal. Sometimes students are so keen they apply for lots of jobs and excitedly take the first one offered. This can lead to disaster if you take an unsuitable post in a school which is desperate to fill its vacancies. It is particularly important that you find a post in a school where you can fit in and feel comfortable.

Beware of the market forces. In times of extreme surplus, highly qualified teachers with top grades in their teaching practices are turned down by dozens of schools, frequently without an acknowledgement. In times of shortage, teachers are given expenses to attend interviews and offered a choice of schools.

At the present time, 2006, we are in a period of shortage in some areas of the state sector, especially in some subjects such as maths and science in secondary schools. If you can offer either of these subjects, you will be shortlisted for every post for which you apply, and quickly snapped up. You may well have the added bonus of about one-tenth of your student loan being deleted for each year that you work in a maintained school. There is also a teacher shortage in some parts of the country, especially the inner cities.

Rising and falling birth rates have a small effect on the number of jobs available. If you are doing the one-year post-graduate course you might take this into consideration, but if you are doing a three-or four-year course, you can ignore it because it will be different by the time you finish. On the whole, teaching is more slump-proof than most professions, because people keep having children regardless.

Availability of jobs varies in different parts of the country and different types of school. Peaceful prep schools can have 30 or more applications for a job, while a school on the council estate, a mile away, can have one or two.

Government policy has more influence than the birth rate on availability of jobs. In recent decades education has fluctuated up and down various governments' lists of priorities. Until recently teachers were treated more sympathetically by Labour than Tory governments, but public opinion governs most things and this could change in the future.

The economy of the country is perhaps the greatest influence. If the money is not made available the jobs disappear. Also in times when graduates are being made redundant from industry, they turn to teaching which is seen as a safe alternative. This is easy for some, because they may have trained as teachers before realizing they could earn substantially more elsewhere. Some schools can be so desperate that they will take teachers without a Post-Graduate Certificate in Education. In prosperous times jobs are easy to find because many graduates go off to industry.

What to consider
Decide on an area of the country where you would ideally like to live. If you are married and/or have children, this is probably already decided for you.

Decide on what type of school – state, independent, inner city or affluent suburb, challenging failed school, satisfactory or out-standing successful school. Of course some are more easy to get jobs in than others.

Even in these secular days, your religion can count. If you are an Anglican, Roman Catholic or Jew, or even a lapsed member of a particular faith, you have a much better chance of finding a job in a school of your chosen (or rejected) faith.

Occasionally you can use whom you know, as well as what you know. Of course you can never openly canvass, but if you have a friend or relation who knows of a school which is looking for a teacher, a quiet word of recommendation can help. Some senior members of staff have told me they try to employ teachers who have been recommended by someone personally known to them.

Do not feel disadvantaged by your youth or inexperience. Both of these are huge points in your favour. Newly qualified equals cheap. Many heads prefer newly qualified teachers because they can save money to redirect towards equipment, books or supply cover. For a head, your inexperience is an added bonus because it is easier to mould a novice into the school's own way of working. An experienced teacher, especially one who has plenty of faith in him/herself, is sometimes seen as a threat by the head who has not spent much time with a class of kids for years, has lost the knack and feels out of touch.

By far the easiest way is to find a job in the school where you do your final teaching practice. Of course this is not always practical because you may not want to stay in the area, but either way, it is worth cultivating the approval of the headteacher, head of department or even class teacher, because you'll need someone who has seen you in operation to write your reference.

If you are unattached to either a partner or a part of the country, and are prepared to go anywhere, one good insurance policy is to find out the area of teacher shortage and apply to that education authority. I acquired my first post after a five-minute interview of uncomplicated questioning in the Inner London Education Authority during the dire shortage in the early 1970s.

At that time, it was practically impossible for a single person to survive on an NQT's salary, and they were leaving in droves. They could rarely find a teacher for every post, and so were accepting almost everyone who applied as well as funding their inter-city train and even aeroplane fares and giving them an allowance towards a day's meals on the day of the interview. The laws of supply and demand are a wonderful thing!

Today, some schools are finding it so difficult they are recruiting from abroad. Some teachers agencies will set up interviews for headteachers on the telephone to teachers in Australia.

Some schools ask teachers to do a brief sample lesson before being interviewed. This mode of assessing candidates has crept in during the last few years and at first caused consternation to older teachers who were unaccustomed to it. Many feel nervous doing it for the first time, but of course there is nothing to worry about, because heads normally give candidates a fairly manageable class, and the pupils are unlikely to misbehave because the head teacher is in the room observing them, as well as the nervous candidate.

In some secondary schools, after the candidate has left the classroom, the pupils are asked to give their opinions and vote on whether they would like him or her to be appointed. Although the pupils do not make the final decision, their views, if canvassed, must be taken into consideration and could make the difference if the interview was mediocre.

Choosing the right school

Choosing the right school is vitally important to passing your induction year. In the past, some newly qualified teachers have spent a miserable first year and failed unnecessarily through not researching the school first. It is now more important than ever because if one fails one's induction year there is no second chance. Happily, few teachers do so.

There are lots of things to check out, most of which can only be done when you visit the school. However before you go, you can do some advance preparation by checking out the following.

The Investors in People Award

This is a prestigious award conferred on schools and other places of work after they have been rigorously inspected. An establishment seeking the Award has to prove that they treat their staff at all levels with care, and provide them with opportunities to progress and develop their skills to benefit their own careers as well as the place of work.

If you apply to a school which bears the Award, it is a sign that the staff are appreciated and treated with respect.

The school's last Ofsted report

As stated previously, every school in the country is inspected about once every four years by Her Majesty's Office for Standards in Education. The inspectors require a load of paperwork to be done in advance, and all your lessons have to be prepared down to the last letter, because each teacher has several lessons observed during the week. Lessons are graded and those whose lessons have consistently high grades are commended, but those whose are consistently poor are in for some unpleasant scrutiny and, in the worst cases, a competence procedure. This is an unpleasant procedure whereby the individual teacher will be inspected and a judgement made as to whether s/he is allowed to continue to work as a teacher. The few teachers whom I know, who were told they would have one, immediately resigned.

There is normally a frenzy of activity before the inspectors appear, and it is quite normal for confident, level-headed teachers to burst into tears, or fall out with colleagues, with whom they usually work in harmony.

A few teachers enjoy the cut and thrust of it but the majority loathe and despise it. They hate it because they suspect that all the extra work and accompanying stress and disruption to their working pattern is a waste of time which does not benefit the children and some would argue that mostly they are right. For some the judgemental aspect gets the whole thing off on the wrong foot. After all, even the most competent teachers have the occasional lesson which goes badly and the thought of one being observed and classified as 'poor' is unnerving to teachers, most of whom care deeply about their credibility. I know of several cases where teachers suffered so much stress that they were ill and in some cases left the school.

For the last several years, every school's most recent general inspection report from Ofsted has been published on the Internet. The website is www.ofsted.gov.uk. It is worth reading it to get an overall picture of the school. If the report is more than three years old, bear in mind that the school may well have changed since its inspection date. Even if you check its SATs or GCE results and find that it has maintained an acceptable position on the league table, do not relax yet. After three years have elapsed, it is due to be re-inspected within the next year! You can find out the date of planned Ofsted inspections on the above website. It is sensible to check before you apply to the school because the first year at the chalk-face is sometimes complicated and stressful enough without the added strain of a visit from representatives of HM Government.

The ideal is to work in a school which has been favourably inspected within the previous year. The atmosphere will be more relaxed and it will be about another three years until Ofsted raises its ugly head and wrecks everyone's private and social life again.

Going into a school which has recently had an unfavourable Ofsted report is attractive to those who are stimulated by a challenge, thrive on pressure and don't value a peaceful life. There is, of course, the advantage that a new teacher is untainted by the failed inspection, since they cannot possibly be blamed for events which took place before their time. Another advantage is that it is easy to find a job in a failed school, although parents and governors will be looking to new teachers with a positive attitude and lots of energy to make substantial improvements. They will expect new teachers to inject the children with enthusiasm which they may have lacked in the past. You can always look on the bright side: once a school has hit the bottom, its only direction is up.

The headteacher

Check if the same head is in situ, because this is the greatest single factor in radical change. Never expect a school to be the same when the head changes. Experienced teachers will tell you they have known schools to change out of all recognition, for good or for ill, in the two years after a new head comes.

Inside information

It helps if you know someone on the inside. Do you know anyone who has done a teaching practice there, worked there, been a pupil or sent their own children there? Only listen to information which is recent because in these fast-moving times the whole ethos and atmosphere of a school can change with alarming speed. Also remember there will be a certain amount of subjectivity in people's comments because every school has its share of staff, pupils and parents who are less content than others.

Know the target

It is usually worth consulting the local league tables, but view them with caution. Schools in wealthy areas with supportive, professional parents should be high up the league. In a school in an impoverished area with large numbers of refugees who do not speak much English, and high mobility of homeless families, it is much more difficult to raise standards and keep them high. If the former type of school is halfway up the table, it is not particularly successful. If the latter is halfway up, it is doing a superb job.

Do not be deterred from working in the latter type. My experience of children who suffer extremes of poverty is that they enjoy coming to school to have something interesting to do. They are frequently willing to work and can be grateful for your efforts, particularly if they cannot speak much English. Recent arrivals in the UK are usually desperate to learn English because they cannot make friends or feel accepted until they do.

Also the staff in this type of school tend to be supportive of each other and so there is often a happy atmosphere in the staffroom. The parents may be unable to support your efforts, but then, they won't be pushy and pressurizing about their children's progress and where they come in the ranking order of the class.

You may however have to cope with a certain amount of aggression from indigenous parents who are resentful of schools in general, sometimes because they got nothing out of education themselves, or have a problem with any kind of authority figure.

In schools in very affluent areas, you may have aggression from demanding, pushy, even snooty, parents, who think they know it all and regard teachers as lesser professionals because of their lower salary. In one extreme case such a parent told me, 'Teachers are the bottom of the pile! That's why they are so badly paid.'

Writing the letter of application

This is most important as heads make their decisions on whether to shortlist on the letter as much as anything. Since this is your first job, you will not be expected to write a very long letter; one or two sides of A4 paper is plenty. Unless the advertisement states otherwise, always type it. One and a half line spacing is suitable. Choose the lecturer with whom you have the best working relationship and ask him/her to be your referee, and ditto for the teacher with whom you had the best relationship on teaching practice for your second referee.

Before you start

Ring up the school and ask them to send you an application form, a school prospectus and a job description and look closely at the details of all three. Every point on the job description must be covered in your letter of application. Make a list of all the points and decide where in the letter you will put each one.

Getting the tone right

This is as important as the content. Remember the head might have lots to choose from and will choose one which sounds enthusiastic over one which sounds matter of fact. You must sound eager as well as serious about the value of the job. Use expressions like:

'I enjoyed my experience as . . . . . .'
'I experienced great satisfaction in learning . . . . . .'
'I learnt a great deal about the value of . . . . . .'
'It has been a privilege to work/study in . . . . . .'
'This is the kind of school where I can contribute a lot . . . . . .'
'It is my goal to make a real difference . . . . . .'

Content and structure

FIRST PARAGRAPH

Start with an introductory sentence stating the post for which you are applying and any reference mentioned in the advertisement. Say which college or university faculty you are studying in at present.

SECOND PARAGRAPH

Try using these points:

- Why you are especially interested in working in that school – you like its ethos, you have read its last Ofsted report and were impressed.
- If it is well up the league tables, say you think it would be 'challenging' (heads like that word) to work in a school with high standards.
- If the school is not high in the league tables, say that you have a special interest in giving opportunity to children who are not advantaged.
- Make sure you address every point which is mentioned in the advertisement. Some heads go through letters with a list, ticking them off as they read them.

THIRD PARAGRAPH

- Tell them about your particular academic strengths and interests, preferably ones which are sought in the advertisement.

- Write about your extra-curricular activities which you can put to good use in the school – football, cricket, any form of music, art or drama, any Combined Cadet Force or adventure type of activity. Heads love teachers who offer extra skills and activities.
- Tell them about your summer jobs or any previous experience of working with children or teenagers and how they have given you useful skills such as organization ability, ability to handle responsibility and being in a position of authority, ability to work amicably in a team.

FINAL PARAGRAPH
Add the names of your referees and finish with a sentence such as:

'I should view this post as in interesting/stimulating challenge.'
'This post would be a valuable opportunity for me to extend my own learning/development/expertise in . . . . . .'

The unofficial interview
If it is a state school, always telephone and ask to come and see the school. Most heads want to meet applicants before the interview and many are sizing them up in preparation for shortlisting. The impression you make at this point is as important as the formal interview. Some heads who have lots of applicants will tell you to wait until the day of the interview, but I have not yet met a state school head who will shortlist a teacher who has not, at least, asked for a visit.

Private school heads take a different stance and will shortlist purely on the basis of the application form or the CV, and the letter of application, and do not normally allow you to visit until the day of the interview.

Look and act the part
Always power dress on the preliminary visit and the interview, whatever you intend wearing for the rest of your life. For men, if not a suit, at least smart trousers and jacket, shirt and tie. Women should wear a suit or smart dress and carry a spare pair of tights in their handbag. If you are going on public transport in heavy rain, a change of shoes would be worth the bother.

Make sure you know the names of the head, and possibly the deputy and/or head of department, and use them. They like that and it creates a good impression. Try to arrive 15 minutes early if you can, but *never* late. Punctuality is so important for teachers. Walk in with your head up, look the head in the eye, and smile confidently.

What to look for
Always visit during the school day to see what the school is really like, because every school looks remarkably peaceful after the pupils go home. While the head is sizing you up, you must look out for and give thought to as many of the following aspects as you can.

THE HEADTEACHER
The head is the greatest single factor influencing any school. Heads set the tone for the school and most of the attitudes and behaviour of the staff can be traced back to him/her.

Is the head friendly and approachable and do you feel comfortable in his/her presence? Does s/he seem interested in you? Would you feel comfortable talking to him/her if you were in difficulty? These are more important in a small school where you will have more direct contact with the head. In a larger school, you will have more contact with heads of department than the head teacher.

As you walk around the school, notice whether s/he speaks pleasantly to the pupils, teachers and other staff. Does s/he allow the staff to use his/her Christian/first name? Nowadays only an older head would still expect to be addressed as Mister, Missis, Miss, except in front of the pupils of course.

THE STAFF
- *Atmosphere.* Try to assess whether the school has a happy, welcoming atmosphere. Do the staff look as if they get on well together and enjoy their work? For me, this is more important than a high place on the league tables.
- *Staff in situ.* Are the other teachers people to whom you can relate? Are there kindred spirits here? Will they help you through the induction year? I know one young teacher who spent her first year in a school where everyone was at least

twenty years older than her. Although everyone was kind to her she often felt lonely and isolated. Some teachers suggest the male/female ratio can affect the atmosphere.

- *Staff turnover*. Ask what is the annual rate of staff turnover. A low percentage rate is an encouraging sign because, unless there is a shortage of jobs, teachers will not stay in a school if it is not a pleasant, happy place. If the turnover is high the head may resent your asking, but this is unlikely to matter because it is probably not a school where you would want to work anyway.

PUPILS

- *In the classroom*. Are they on task, polite and reasonably interested in their work?
- *In the corridors*. Does their standard of behaviour slip as soon as they walk out of the structured environment of the classroom?
- *Playground behaviour*. Try to see if there are any fights in the playground. I would consider a harmonious playground a higher priority than SATs/GCSE results, although it is of course worth looking at those as well.
- *Out of school* – in the street, at bus-stops, in the buses (secondary). I think pupils' true selves appear when they are completely unsupervised.
- *Noise levels*. Check the noise levels in classrooms. Is it a noise of positive activity or just plain rowdy?
- *Behaviour policy*. As you walk around a primary school look out for charts with children's names, stars and stickers. Ask the head what incentive schemes and reward systems they use. It is sensible for a school to have a few positive ways of encouraging children, but if they have lots of them, tread carefully because that usually means that the children are difficult to motivate and there are difficulties with behaviour management. In a secondary school, notice if there is an Honours Board or any other notice-boards with information or newspaper clippings of pupils' achievements. Is there a display cabinet with cups, trophies or shields? These are always a positive sign. And of course, don't forget to admire them.

THE JOB

- *Pupil/teacher relationships*. How do they interact? In harmony or confrontationally?
- *The styles of teaching*. Are they conventional, progressive, practical, creative, boring? Is there much freedom of teaching style, is it prescribed and is it a format into which you can fit comfortably?
- *What the job demands*. Remember, interviews are a two-way process. Teachers often forget that they need to assess whether the school is right for them. A helpful headteacher will try to give you plenty of information about everything which the job requires. Don't be afraid to ask questions.
- *The extra clauses*. Check what overnight school journeys you will have to go on, and if there are any Saturday commitments.

THE ETHOS OF THE SCHOOL

If the school has to cater for a wide range of races, classes and creeds it is a definite point in the school's favour if all the races mix harmoniously. This can only be achieved in an atmosphere of tolerance and mutual respect. It is impossible in a short visit to gauge this fully, but you might notice the following:

- Is the multiracial aspect of the school population reflected in the displays?
- Are Muslim girls and Sikh boys allowed to wear veils and patkas – a gauge of the school's ethos of tolerance?
- Does the art work reflect each culture?
- Is there music from different cultures?
- Does the racial mix of the staff differ greatly from that of the pupils or are there some teachers or non-teaching staff who can speak the language of some of the pupils? (This point must be viewed cautiously as many schools try hard but are unable to find suitable staff with the right mother tongue.)
- Is there a policy of speaking English only in a multiracial school? Are pupils allowed to speak their own language among themselves or, more importantly, are bilingual pupils encouraged to interpret for new pupils who are still in the process of learning English?

THE PRACTICAL EVERYDAY ISSUES

Parking space. Don't underestimate its importance. It is annoying to find yourself in an inner city school with no on-site or street parking and so you have to come on public transport, which may add an hour's tedium to each end of your working day.

Name policy. Never address the head by Christian/first name until you are sure it's the acceptable thing to do. In a few schools the staff are still not allowed to do so. In others, the children address the staff, even the head, by their Christian/first names. This can be important to some teachers who have strong feelings on the subject.

Lunch time arrangements. Are the staff expected to eat in the dining hall with the pupils, and the noise? It can give you a headache after a frustrating morning and leave you less fit for the afternoon's challenges. Do they give you a free lunch if you eat there? Is the food edible? This is not a trivial issue. A nutritious midday meal and a break are important to many teachers so as to be on form in the afternoon.

The dress code. There are still some schools where men have to wear a smart shirt and tie and I have even heard of a school where women were given a hard time if they wore trousers. Muslim women teachers especially need to check if it is acceptable to wear a veil. You could avoid the problem by showing up for the interviews wearing what is right for you as there would be no point in a fuss being made after you are appointed. If you make it clear you will be wearing your traditional dress to work, they will only employ you if they find that acceptable. In any case who would want to work in atmosphere of intolerance anyway?

Religious holidays. If you will want to have time off, for example for Jewish or Muslim festivals, it is best to ask before appointed as it can cause grief if you leave it until close to the event and are refused. When offered a post is a good time to ask. Also, if you are Jewish and need to leave school before sundown on Fridays, tell the head about that in advance. Of course, you can soften it by saying something like, 'I am happy to do anything after school Monday to Thursday, but on Fridays I do need to leave promptly'.

The official interview

After reading the application forms and meeting candidates, the head and governors select a shortlist for interviewing formally.

Remember that interviews are a two-way process: you are finding out about the job as much as they are finding out about you. Everyone has their own priority. Mine is to ensure that the head and teachers are people that I feel I can trust and work with amicably.

It is not enough to give the right answers, they also want teachers who are pleasant company and can form satisfactory relationships with adults and children. They know you are inexperienced but will probably allow for that if you show enthusiasm and commitment to your career.

If you are applying for a secondary post it is essential to study the NC document for your subject(s) as they will be eager to know if your knowledge and understanding are sound. If the post is in a primary school, they will focus on the curricula for the age group where you will be working, so an hour or two reminding yourself of its content is time well spent.

You can expect to be asked at least some of the questions listed below so it's wise to smoothe the path for yourself by writing short essay type answers once you have been shortlisted. The night before your interview ask a friend to read your questions to give you a practice interview. Read your answers about an hour before the interview to refresh your memory.

The questions will vary depending on the type of school and the needs of the children. Sometimes questions are designed to find out how you would cope in certain circumstances. Often an NQT cannot possibly know exactly what to do because they do not have the required experience, but it is important that you show the confidence and common sense to seek advice and guidance and are willing to learn. So don't worry if you do not always have the perfect answer for every situation.

Likely questions and a few suggested answers

Primary
Q How would you organize your class?
A Prepare some notes explaining how you would organize the class for different subjects, emphasizing the need for variety according to the needs of the children and the demands of the subject.

Describe how you would have a system for giving pupils responsibility for looking after books and equipment and keeping areas of the classroom tidy. Tell them how you would have differentiated ability groups for maths, and mixed groups for practical subjects like science and PE, especially if there are pupils in the early stages of learning English.

Q   How would you set up your classroom?

A   You can start by saying that you are acutely aware that the environment has a strong effect on behaviour. Your aim would be to make the classroom an attractive, stimulating place with colourful displays of pupils' work to encourage them, and show that teachers consider their achievements important.

Also point out that convenience reduces frustration and so equipment should be accessible to the pupils, who should be trained to put everything in its place, preferably labelled, when not in use. Say you are aware of the importance of pupils being seated where they can comfortably see the board or interactive whiteboard (if you are lucky!).

Add in a comment about the need to seat pupils with others with whom they can work amicably.

Q   How would you extend the more able and support the less able?

A   Make it clear you are aware of the wide difference in pupils' abilities, and levels of English if it is a multicultural school, and so the need for differentiation of work – extension work for the more able, simplified work for the less able. Point out that a large part of helping pupils to achieve is tied up with making the lessons fun. There are plenty of maths games on the market for pupils of all abilities, to make the subject enjoyable and give lots of extra practice at each level to enable them to acquire concepts painlessly. There are also lots of sets of books of short playscripts which pupils of different levels can enjoy reading in parts together.

Add that a large part of getting the best out of pupils of all levels is making the subject real. The best way to do this is to back up the Literacy Hour with an occasional educational trip. There is nothing like seeing a film or theatre production of a play or novel to make the print come off the page and enthral the reluctant reader. A trip to a historical site with 'hands-on' activities always raises the enthusiasm levels and the quality of writing produced after the event.

Q How do you view the role of the nursery nurse/the classroom assistant? (Infants)

A You could explain that nursery nurses are semi-professional people with proper training for the post so they must be given trust and responsibility which matches their skills. They should be included in the planning and delivery of the curriculum. A teacher should find out what the nursery nurse's skills are and make best use of them. Also, as professionals, nursery nurses have got to grow and develop like everyone else. They must be given opportunities to go on courses and learn new skills and use the training for the pupils' benefit. Classroom assistants vary enormously. Some have very few qualifications and some have degrees. Although in the past, CAs only did the trivial jobs, today they are given more responsibility and allowed to teach small groups. Although they should be encouraged to extend their skills by going on courses, teachers should not take advantage of them. They should not be expected to plan lessons on their own and on no account should one leave them alone with the class.

Q How would you set about supporting pupils in your lessons who spoke very little or no English?

A If you speak the language of any of the pupils, for example Urdu or Cantonese, you are at great advantage. Say that you would start by consulting the EAL teacher for advice about what they can do and reading the pupils' EAL records. Emphasize the value of mother tongue teaching. Ask if they have any mother tongue teachers or assistants or any bilingual texts in the school. These ideas should help:

- In Key Stage 1, allow the pupil lots of opportunities to indulge in imaginative play, as infants pick up language so quickly.
- Start each lesson by explaining the keywords for the lesson. This also helps some of the English-speaking pupils.
- As far as possible put EAL pupils next to bilingual pupils who can translate for them and encourage the bilinguals to support their classmates.

- Similarly, if it is difficult or impossible for them to grasp new concepts with unfamiliar language, e.g. in maths, it is fair practice to ask a capable bilingual pupil to explain work in the child's mother tongue.
- Always organize the timetable so that they have practical lessons like science and technology when the EAL support teacher is in the classroom to support them.
- Involve them in collaborative tasks where they will work with English-speaking pupils who can be good role models for them.
- Give them the opportunity to access the same lessons as the rest of the class by simplifying the worksheets to their level. EAL pupils learn better in practical lessons.
- Build into lessons opportunities to practise speaking.
- When EAL pupils start to read, they need a lot of practice so it works well to ask competent readers in the class to listen to them reading for five or ten minutes each day.

Secondary

Q   Give an example of how you have got pupils interested and excited about your subject.

A   Say you believe that pupils are best excited by giving them lessons which are fun. Point out how school trips can raise the interest level and make a subject come alive. Pupils almost always produce a better quality of work after a day trip.

Pupils also prefer subjects that are relevant to their lives. It is always worthwhile showing pupils areas in their lives in which they can use the information or skill.

Variety is the spice of life. Use visual, auditory and kinaesthetic methods. Pupils love hands-on activities. Put in a few examples which are appropriate to your subject. Try to present work in a variety of ways, and give pupils opportunities to engage in active learning and finding things out for themselves.

Q   What behaviour management strategies would you use?

A   Say you would like to read the school's behaviour policy and of course realize you have to fit in with it. In addition, you think it would be good practice to discuss class rules with the class at the outset and have a set of rules to which everyone agrees, if that fits in with the school ethos. Explain that you would like to have a system of rewards and sanctions, and you believe a lot of misbehaviour can be avoided by making sure it is clear to pupils what is needed in terms of punctuality, home-work completed on time. Add that it is important that teach-ers speak politely and respectfully to pupils because sarcasm and cutting remarks provoke pupils into misbehaving.

Q   How would you include the classroom assistants (CAs) in your planning?

A   Suggest that you could provide the CA with differentiated work and go through the lesson plan orally beforehand to make sure it is clear to him/her.

Q   All teachers are expected to contribute to extra-curricular activities. How do you see yourself contributing?

A   Describe what you can do – Duke of Edinburgh Award Scheme, Combined Cadet Force, amateur dramatics, or what-ever. Add that you are willing to do so in the future but for the first term or two you would like to establish yourself and get the teaching load under control. (Never promise to start extra-curricular activities earlier because it is just too much for an NQT – once you have promised to do it you cannot back out without creating a lot of ill-feeling.)

Q   Teamwork is important for the smooth running of the depart-ment. Why do you think you would be able to fit in well?

A   Agree wholeheartedly. Say how you worked in collaboration with others in other jobs you have had – unqualified teaching, working in a youth centre, working in an office or other career before teaching. If appropriate, say you have met the rest of the team and liked them and are sure you could get on with them or would welcome the opportunity to do so.

Q   If a pupil asked you a subject knowledge question and you did not know the answer, how would you respond?

A   Respond by explaining that you would not be afraid to say, 'I don't know. That's a good question. I'll definitely find out for you,' and of course it must be followed through by the next lesson.

Q   How would you set about including pupils who spoke very little or no English in your lesson planning?

A   Say you would consult the EAL coordinator to find out more about their level of attainment, and get advice on how to differentiate the work for them. Talk to the EAL support teacher and plan the lesson with him/her. Give the EAL pupils a sheet with the keywords and meanings to keep on their desk as a reference. Use the list of suggestions in the 'Primary' section above.

Q   If a pupil with a diagnosed learning difficulty was causing a habitual disturbance in the classroom, what would you do?

A   Say you would consult the special educational needs coordinator (SENCO) for help and advice. It would of course depend on whether the pupil was able to help him/herself. The pupil may need extra classroom support or it may be the case that the pupil was perfectly capable of behaving acceptably but was taking advantage of your being new. It would be wise to consult the parents, who are often able to give support.

Q   If a parent telephones and demands dictatorially to see you immediately school is over, what do you do?

A   Make clear that you would endeavour not to show alarm under such circumstances. If you had another school commitment after lessons say what it is – staff meeting, appointment with another parent, after-school club, and offer to see the parents after that. If they refuse offer 7.30 or 8 o' clock the following morning. If you had a personal appointment, e.g. dental appointment, say it is not possible but offer early the next morning. Tell the parent that if it is urgent they should look to talk to the head of department. Keep the HOD informed and ask him/her to be present when you meet an aggressive parent. You would try above all to let the parent realize that you were not prepared to be pushed around.

Q   How would you deal with a pupil who almost never did their homework?

A   Suggest giving the pupil a warning that they will have to stay in at lunch time and do it, or that you would be telephoning his/her parents and asking them to ensure the work is done. Then carry it through. Ask if this fits in with their school policy.

Q   How would you deal with a pupil who is consistently late?

A   Give a warning that the time they are late will be made up by being kept back in the classroom at break-time, and follow it through. Again ask about the school's policy.

Primary or secondary

Q   What made you choose this school?

A   This is a chance to pay them a compliment, e.g. you like its
    ethos or friendly atmosphere, or you have heard favourable
    reports about the school from friends or parents. You have read
    their last Ofsted report or noticed that they were high on the
    league tables and you are impressed. Add that you want to
    work in a school where the pupils are conscientious and would
    find it stimulating to work in a school where standards are
    already high.

    Conversely, it is just as valid to say that you would find it stim-
    ulating to work in a school where the pupils present challenges.
    You could say that the post offered exactly the type of experi-
    ence you most want, or you want to develop a certain skill for
    which this post would give you an opportunity.

    If you live close to the school, never say that its proximity is
    your first, second or even third reason. They are looking for
    teachers who are interested in the school; not their own con-
    venience. However you could add at the end that having no
    accommodation or travel problems would enable you to devote
    more time and energy to the job.

Q   What skills and qualities can you bring to this school?

A   Have a list ready – boundless energy, ambition, eagerness to
    succeed in the profession, a strong interest in achieving progress,
    the experience of bringing up children, working with children
    in youth groups, and if you live locally an interest in or thor-
    ough knowledge of the neighbourhood and the community.

Q   How would you deal with disruptive pupils?
    (Beware of the school where you are asked this one because it
    often means they have too many of them.)

A   Say that first you would like to read the school's policy for
    dealing with it. Then you can add that it is important to find
    out the reasons before you can decide how to deal with it.

    • It may be that the child is frustrated because they can never
      do the work and so you can suggest that they have their
      own scheme of work and you may even have to give them
      a few minutes of individual attention at the start of the
      lesson to ensure they can achieve something.

- If the child has a reading difficulty, it is important that they are assessed for dyslexia, because this condition can lead to great frustration and antisocial behaviour if left undiagnosed.
- The child may be a refugee or asylum seeker and be shell-shocked by suddenly having to cope in an unfamiliar culture. They may be literally shell-shocked, as some refugees have suffered appalling wartime hardships, in which case they may need counselling and a large helping of sympathy and encouragement.
- It may simply be that the child is spoilt rotten and cannot come to terms with not having their own way all the time, in which case you just have to clamp down and tell the child that if they waste the class's valuable lesson time, you will waste their break-time (or equivalent), and do carry it out.
- Also talk to the parents. If approached tactfully, making it clear that you are most concerned about the child's progress, they may well be supportive.

Q   Explain the different stages of the special needs register.

A   This changes so often that anything I could write would be out of date by the time the book appears on the shelf. You have to look at the up-to-date information at the time.

Q   Imagine the inspector is coming and you have to present a model lesson and you want to impress. Describe what you would do.

A   Describe a lesson where there was much successful active learning.

Q   Describe a scheme of lessons which you prepared and delivered when on teaching practice and which worked well.

A   As the previous question. Have the answer prepared mentally. Explain your objectives, the activities, and how you ensured that the less able were able to participate and the more able were extended.

Q   How would you ensure inclusion?

A   Ask them about the school's policy before you dive in. Say that it is important to differentiate the work so that pupils of lower ability can take part in lessons even it they cannot achieve as high a standard as the rest.

Say you would use the support staff for pupils with special needs or who may be in the early stages of learning English, because they are there to enable pupils to cope with areas of the curriculum where they might normally find it difficult to keep up with the rest of the class. Support teachers should also be involved in the planning of lessons and you would encourage them to stay in the classroom and support the pupils while they have the same lesson as the rest of the class, even if their work is pitched at a lower level.

If there is no support teacher available, where possible let children carry out practical work in mixed ability groups because children do learn from each other.

Q   Is there anything you would like to ask about the school?

A   Always have something ready to ask so that it looks as if you have thought about it. You could ask any of these questions:

How will the staff here help me through the induction year?

What are the school's main strengths?

What are they focusing on improving at the moment?

How supportive are the parents?

What percentage of children are on the special needs register/ EAL register?

The closing question

Q   If you were offered the post, would you accept it?

A   (This question means that they have not ruled you out.)

Often people do not make up their minds that they want a post until the interview. It is not unusual for applicants to change their minds during the interview.

If you want the post then just say 'Yes'. At the end, shake hands, thank them for the interview and look happy.

Things to consider

You might want the post but may want to negotiate on pay, in which case, I should wait until the head telephones you to offer it, then say that you would love to accept the post as long as your other experience is recognized in the terms. If you are applying for a post in a shortage subject you may well be in a strong position to negotiate.

If you have had teaching experience before your PGCE you can reasonably ask them to acknowledge that in the salary point. If you have done the course as a mature student having had a previous career they are often willing to give you some credit for that. Always ask for your other experience to be considered, in a polite and respectful manner. If you become aggressive or high-handed about it you may deter the head from employing you and risk losing the job. If the terms are not what you want then you will just have to decide between accepting it and trying to find a better paid post.

If you have applied for another post or are waiting for a reply from a previous interview, and are then offered another post, honesty is the best policy. Say that you want to hear from the other school before making a response and indicate when you expect to hear from them. They may or may not allow you the time but they will appreciate your honesty. It will count in your favour and show them that someone else is interested in you.

If you have said in the interview that you would take the post but then turn it down when offered it there is a possibility that the head will pass on your name to other local heads as a teacher who does not do as they say they will do. Sometimes colleges are contacted and told that students have not stuck to their word.

Finally accepting a job

This is a great relief because it enables you to study for your final exams or complete the final placement without stress, but beware, the job is conditional upon you passing your exams and school placements successfully.

Supply Teaching in your School at the End of the Summer Term

Starting in a new school is always a steep learning curve for the first few weeks even if you are an experienced teacher because each school is unique. The learning curve is even steeper if you are an NQT.

Heads normally invite NQTs to do some supply work in the school at the end of the summer term after their course is finished.

If the head does not invite you to do so, I should ask if it is possible. Even if the answer is no, s/he will be pleased that you are keen. It is an opportunity to get to know the staff, pupils, the geography and general workings and ease yourself in gently.

If it is a wealthy school, you may be very lucky and they will put you on the payroll throughout the summer holidays for working for some of June and July. At the very least, try to go to the school for a day or two before the end of the summer term.

When you start
NQTs are often excited and nervous at the same time. After all your hard work you are actually on the threshold of your working life and about to be paid for it as well. These weeks are so important because you will be laying the foundation for your induction year, which of course you have to pass.

A few tips
Mind how you go

- Dress as smartly as everyone else on the staff.
- Arrive at school at the same time as most of the staff.

Don't tread on toes

- Some NQTs try to hide their nerves by acting smart. Teachers are never fooled by it and it rubs them up the wrong way.
- Keep any particularly strong views to yourself until you are established in the school. I have known new teachers to find themselves isolated after they have irritated everyone with their criticisms and suggestions for improvement.
- Don't get into disagreements with your colleagues on educational matters. Keep the path smooth.
- If you are being paid for the summer holidays as well as the days you work, don't advertise it to others. There may be a teacher who was not given the same privilege.
- Strictly no school politics. It's more trouble than it is worth but keep your ears open. Knowing about underlying staff conflicts helps you to avoid getting involved in them.

Building relationships

- Chat to the support staff at breaks and get to know them.
- Be willing to learn from other teachers with experience. Don't be afraid to ask anything you don't know. They will be pleased you are eager to learn, but be aware how busy they are.
- Make sure you go to the staffroom at break-times. You'll be surprised how much more relaxed you will feel and how much better you will perform after a cup of tea and a snack, and it's always an opportunity to seek help if you need it and to get to know your colleagues.
- If staff invite you to the pub after school, do go, even if you do not drink alcohol.
- Make friends with any other NQTs in the school, because you will need each other's support in the busy year ahead.
- Try to establish a friendly rapport with your mentor (primary) or head of department (secondary) and be willing to defer to him/her. Remember s/he can be a tower of strength to you and will be the one to assess your performance and decide if you pass or fail your induction year.
- Stay on the right side of the head!
- Acknowledge to your colleagues that you are benefiting from their help. Make them feel it is worth your time being there and their time helping you.

Be proactive – show willing

- Offer to do playground duties.
- If you are asked to go into a class to observe how things are done, offer to be involved with the lesson.

In a primary school the head usually asks you to go into the classroom with the class which you will have the following year and their present teacher. This is a great chance to get to know them before you start. It also sets your mind at ease and stops you worrying for the summer. Try to find opportunities to ask the teacher at least some of the following:

- what discipline strategies work well;
- which children are most difficult to manage and what they respond to;
- what support the children get for special needs and English as an additional language, if appropriate;
- which parents are supportive, which are not and which are hostile;
- which incentives work best.

Sometimes the absentee rate among teachers increases at the end of the academic year so the head might use you as a supply to cover their classes. This is often difficult as you can spend a fortnight being pushed from one end of the school to the other and having a different class every day.

If in a primary school you are asked to teach an age group for which you are not trained you may be tempted to try to get out of it but it will enhance your credibility better if you don't. If you are nervous about it try saying, 'I don't mind having a go, but you know I have no training for that age group. Is there someone who could show me what work they are doing and help me get something ready for them?' This of course is another reason to be in early. If you are told at 7.45 in the morning what class you will have, you will be better prepared and feel more confident than if you have come rushing in at 8.45.

It won't matter too much if a day spent with an unfamiliar age group is not very successful; they will be so pleased you were willing to try that it will not be held against you.

In a secondary school during this period you may be asked to write some schemes of work or revamp old ones or cover classes for absent teachers. If asked to cover a class for a subject other than your own, there should be work left. If not, ask the relevant head of department for work.

During these weeks it is not so important to shine as a teacher. Your main aim is to become familiar with the school, its way of working and to get to know the staff and pupils and, more importantly than you might imagine, to establish a positive working relationship with the head. If you achieve that you will have laid a firm foundation for a very successful induction year and should pass with flying colours.

Supply teaching elsewhere

Sometimes heads do not want to employ you at the end of the term or, more likely, they are unable to pay you. If this is the case it is worthwhile finding some supply work anyway so as to quickly gain some experience and earn some extra money.

It is quite difficult to be a supply teacher at the end of the summer term because the pupils are tired and looking forward to the end of the year, so don't worry if it does not go as well as you hope. It is always different in September.

There is a list of names and contact details of supply teaching agencies in Appendix 3 to help you find work.

Appendix 1

Abbreviations and acronyms

ADHD	Attention deficit hyperactivity disorder
A-levels	Advanced Levels
ATL	Association of Teachers and Lecturers
BA	Bachelor of Arts
B.Ed.	Bachelor of Education
CA	Classroom assistant
CV	Curriculum vitae
DfES	Department for Education and Skills
EAL	English as an Additional Language
EIS	Educational Institute of Scotland
EP	Educational Psychologist
EWO	Educational Welfare Officer
GCSE	General Certificate of Secondary Education
GTTP	Graduate Teacher Training Programme
HM	Her Majesty's (Government)
HOD	Head of Department
ICT	Information and Communications Technology
IEP	Individualized Educational Programme
INSET	In-service Education of Teachers
INTO	Irish National Teachers' Organization
LEA	Local Education Authority
NASUWT	National Association of Schoolmasters and Union of Women Teachers
NC	National Curriculum
NFER	National Foundation for Educational Research
NOF	New Opportunities Funding (for computer training)
NUT	National Union of Teachers
NQT	Newly qualified teacher
Ofsted	Office for Standards in Education
PAT	Professional Association of Teachers
PE	Physical Education

PGCE	Post-Graduate Certificate in Education
PSHE	Personal, Social and Health Education
QCA	Qualifications and Curriculum Authority
QTS	Qualified Teacher Status
RE	Religious Education
SAT	Standardized Assessment Tests
SCITT	School Centred Initial Teacher Training
SEN	Special Educational Needs
SENCO	Special Educational Needs Coordinator
SSSS	Secondary Shortage Subject Scheme
TP	Teaching Practice
UCAS	Universities and Colleges Admissions Services
UTU	Ulster Teachers' Union

Appendix 2

Teachers' Unions and Associations
Contact details
Association of Teachers and Lecturers (ATL)
7 Northumberland Street, London WC2N 5RD
Tel: 020 7930 6441   Fax: 0207 930 1359
Email: info@atl.org.uk   Website: www.atl.org.uk
(171,000 members)

Educational Institute of Scotland (EIS)
46 Moray Place, Edinburgh EH3 6BH
Tel: 0131 225 6244   Fax: 0131 220 3151
Email: enquiries@eis.org.uk   Website: www.eis.org.uk
(50,000 members)

Irish National Teachers' Organization (INTO)
23 College Gardens, Belfast BT9 6BS
Tel: 028 9038 1455   Fax: 028 9066 2803
Email: info@ni.ie   Website: www.into.ie
(6,000 members)

Irish National Teachers' Organization (INTO) in the Republic of Ireland
35 Parnell Square, Dublin 1
Tel: +353 1 8047700   Fax: +353 1 8722462
Email: info@into.ie   Website: www.into.ie
(31,000 members)

National Association of Schoolmasters & Union of Women Teachers (NASUWT)
Hillscourt Education Centre, Rose Hill, Rednal, Birmingham BS4 8RS
Tel: 0121 453 6150   Fax: 0121 457 6208/6209
Email: membership@mail.nasuwt.org.uk
nasuwt@mail.nassuwt.org.uk
Website: www.teachersunion.org.uk
(234,000 members)

NASUWT in Scotland
6 Waterloo Place, Edinburgh, EH1 3BG
Tel: 0131 5231110   Fax: 0131 5231119
Email: rc-scotland@mail.nasuwt.org.uk
Website: www.teachersunion.org.uk

NASUWT in Wales
NASUWT Cymru, Greenwood Close, Cardiff Gate Business Park,
Cardiff CF23 8RD
Tel: 029 2054 6080   Fax: 029 2054 6089
Email: rc-wales-cymru@mail.nasuwt.org.uk

National Union of Teachers (NUT)
Hamilton House, Mabledon Place, London WC1H 9BD
Tel: 020 7380 4747   Fax: 020 7387 8458 Membership
hotline 0845 300 1669
Website: www.teachers.org.uk
(248,000 members)

Professional Association of Teachers (PAT)
2 St James' Court, Friar Gate, Derby DE1 1BT
(For teachers in England and Wales)
Tel: 01332 372337   Fax: 01332 290310
Email: hq@pat.org.uk   Website: www.pat.org.uk
(43,000 members)

Professional Association of Teachers in Scotland
1–3 Colne Street, Edinburgh EH3 6AA
(for teachers in Scotland and Northern Ireland)
Tel: 0131 220 8241 and 0131 317 8282   Fax: 0131 220 8350
Email: scotland@pat.org.uk   Website: www.pat.org.uk

Scottish Secondary Teachers' Association (SSTA)
15 Dundas Street, Edinburgh EH3 6QG
Tel: 0131 556 5919   Fax: 0131 556 1419
Email: info@ssta.org.uk   Website: www.ssta.org.uk
(7,000 members)

Ulster Teachers Union (UTU)
94 Malone Road, Belfast BT9 5HP
Tel: 028 9066 2216   Fax: 028 9068 3296
Email: office@utu.edu   Website: www.utu.edu
(7,000 members)

Appendix 3

Supply teaching agencies
Associated Education
Tel: 01643 707085
Email: kerryevans@btconnect.org
Somerset and Devon

Career teachers
Tel: 020 7382 4270 and 0845 8800950
Email: info@careerteachers.co.uk
London

Capita Education Resourcing
Tel: 0800 731 6871 (Primary); 0800 731 6872 (Secondary);
0800 731 6873 (SEN); 0800 316 1332 (Further Education)
Email: ers@capita.co.uk
Branches nationwide

Celsian:education
Tel: 0845 606 0676
Email: enquiries@celsiangroup.co.uk
Branches nationwide

Class Act Teaching Services
Tel: 0800 028 6196
Email: classact@teachingservices.fsnet.co.uk
Hertfordshire, Oxfordshire, Warwickshire, Yorkshire

Concorde Teaching Bank
Tel: 01872 262033
Email: concordeteachingbank@cornwall.ac.uk
Cornwall and Isles of Scilly

Cover Teachers
Tel: 0117 973 5695
Email: enquiries@coverteachers.co.uk
South-West England

Education Recruitment Network
Tel: 01633 223747
Email: erninfo@aol.com
Wales, Southern England and Jersey

Hays Education
Tel: 0800 716026
Email: enquiries@hays-education.com
England and Wales

ITN Teachers
Tel: 020 7246 4777
Email: admin@itnteachers.com
London and Home Counties

Key Stage Teacher Supply
Tel: 01254 298616
Email: info@keystagesupply.co.uk
East Lancashire and M65 corridor

Link Education
Tel: 0845 130 4586
Email: linkeducation@btconnect.com
Kent, Essex, Bexley, Bromley

Longterm Teachers
Tel: 0845 130 6149
Email: info@longtermteachers.com
England

Mark Education
Tel: 01534 62112
Email: info@markeducation.co.uk
England and Wales

Marverose
Tel: 0870 4294845
Email: marveroseteachers@safe-mail.net
South-East England and abroad

Masterlock Recruitment
Tel: 0117 915 4567 West Country; 020 7229 6699 London and
Home Counties
Email: info@masterlock.co.uk

Protocol Teachers
Tel: 020 8515 6655 and 0845 450 9450
Email: info@protocolteachers.com
Text: 81025 'teach' name and postcode
Branches nationwide

Quality Teacher Recruitment
Tel: 0800 783 7405
Email: qtr@supplyteaching.com
Norfolk

Quay Education Services
Tel: 020 7535 3039 East London; 020 8563 8885 West London; 0114
273 1616 Sheffield
Fax: 0113 383 3745 Leeds
Email: teach@quayeducation.co.uk; educate@quayeducation.co.uk;
learn@quayeducation.co.uk; develop@quayeducation.co.uk

Renaissance Education
Tel: 020 7712 1577
Email: teach@edulon.co.uk
South London

Select Education
Tel: 0845 600 1234
Email: education@selecteducation.com
Branches nationwide

Standby Teachers
Tel: 0800 146471
Email: info@standbyteachers.com
Yorkshire

Teachers UK
Tel: 0800 068 1117
Email: education@teachers-uk.co.uk
London and Home Counties

Teaching Life 5
Tel: 0800 781 4572
Email: teachinglife5@aol.com
North-West London, Luton, Hertfordshire, Birmingham, Cambridge

Termwise Teacher Recruitment
Tel: 01305 268565
Email: info@termwise.co.uk
London and Home Counties

Timeplan
Tel: 0800 358 8040
Email: tes@timeplan.net
England and Scotland

Trust Education
Tel 020 7328 0000
Email: info@trusteducation.co.uk
London

Appendix 4

Suggested further reading and Bibliography

FURTHER READING

Bennett, H. (2005) *The Ultimate Teacher's Handbook*. Continuum International.

Bowden, D., Gray, B. and Thody, A. (2004) *The Teacher's Survival Guide 2nd edition*. Continuum International.

Bubb, S. (2003) *The Insider's Guide for New Teachers*. Kogan Page.

Cowley, S. (2003) *Guerilla Guide to Teaching*. Continuum International.

Cowley, S. (2003) *How to Survive the First Year of Teaching*. Continuum International.

BIBLIOGRAPHY

Fine, A. (1992) *The chicken gave it to me*. London: Egmont.

Marryat, F. (1874) *The children of the New Forest*. Massachussetts: Kessinger Publishing Co.

Shakespeare, W. (c1606) *King Lear*. Cambridge: Cambridge University Press.

Index

Whole chapters are in **bold**